Gender, Sex and Children's Play

ALSO AVAILABLE FROM BLOOMSBURY

Reflective Playwork, Jacky Kilvington and Ali Wood
Rethinking Gender and Sexuality in Childhood, Emily W. Kane
Rethinking Children's Play, Fraser Brown and Michael Patte

Gender, Sex and Children's Play

JACKY KILVINGTON AND ALI WOOD

Bloomsbury Academic
An imprint of Bloomsbury Publishing Plc

B L O O M S B U R Y
LONDON · OXFORD · NEW YORK · NEW DELHI · SYDNEY

Bloomsbury Academic

An imprint of Bloomsbury Publishing Plc

50 Bedford Square	1385 Broadway
London	New York
WC1B 3DP	NY 10018
UK	USA

www.bloomsbury.com

BLOOMSBURY and the Diana logo are trademarks of Bloomsbury Publishing Plc

First published 2016

© Jacky Kilvington and Ali Wood, 2016

British Library Cataloguing-in-Publication Data

A catalogue record for this book is available from the British Library.

ISBN:	HB:	978-1-4725-2857-5
	PB:	978-1-4725-2458-4
	ePDF:	978-1-4725-3163-6
	ePub:	978-1-4725-2356-3

Library of Congress Cataloging-in-Publication Data

Names: Wood, Ali, author. | Kilvington, Jacky, author.
Title: Gender, sex and children's play / Ali Wood and Jacky Kilvington.
Description: London ; New York : Bloomsbury Academic, 2016. | Includes bibliographical references and index.
Identifiers: LCCN 2016005872 (print) | LCCN 2016013809 (ebook) | ISBN 9781472524584 (paperback) | ISBN 9781472528575 (hb) | ISBN 9781472531636 (epdf) | ISBN 9781472523563 (epub)
Subjects: LCSH: Play. | Sex role. | Sex differences. | Child development. | BISAC: EDUCATION / General. | EDUCATION / Preschool & Kindergarten. | EDUCATION / Educational Psychology.
Classification: LCC LB1137 .W66 2016 (print) | LCC LB1137 (ebook) | DDC 372.21–dc23
LC record available at http://lccn.loc.gov/2016005872

Cover design by Terry Woodley
Cover image © PeopleImages.com / Getty Images

Typeset by Fakenham Prepress Solutions, Fakenham, Norfolk NR21 8NN

To all our grandchildren – Ellie, Josh, Beth, Dylan, Owen, Sam, Ethan and Jessica

CONTENTS

TABLES AND ILLUSTRATIONS

Tables

Figures

ACKNOWLEDGEMENTS

We owe thanks to a number of people but our biggest thanks go to Jess Milne who conducted workshops with Ali, about children, sexuality and play – without him this book would have been less. We would also like to offer thanks to all the people who have attended any of our workshops about gender, sex and play – their contributions have added much to our thinking and knowledge about 'real life' experience, which has helped contextualize the 'research that we have researched'. A big thank you to the adventure playgrounds, after school clubs and school playgrounds and the playworkers and playground supervisors who work in them, but especially the children who play in them, from whom we have collected 'evidence' of children playing in the here and now.

We would like to give special thanks to the children whose play stories or pictures appear in the book – we hope we have done your playing justice.

Thanks are also due to Pete, Dave and Steve for their technical help. Finally, we would like to thank each other – writing the book together has been very life affirming.

PREFACE

How did we come to write this book? In 2006, we, and other female playworkers, noticed most of the influential writers that informed the theory and philosophy behind playwork were men; at that time, we believed this biased their thinking. This resulted in our first writing and we had a chapter, 'The Gentle Art of Agonism – Speculations and Possibilities of Missing Female Perspectives', published in *Playwork Voices* (2007), a book to celebrate the work of two revered male playwork theorists, Bob Hughes and Gordon Sturrock. In it, using Else's *Integral Play Framework* (2003) in which to locate our arguments, we outlined why we thought there might be missing female perspectives in playwork theory and we presented four areas in which we felt there needed to be a more female voice. One of these was 'Gender and Play'. In that chapter, we asked a number of questions, some of which we are still pursuing today.

That chapter was followed by another in *Foundations of Playwork* (2008) entitled 'The Enigma of the Missing Female Perspective in Playwork Theory' in which we outlined potential differences between male and female brains, thinking and communicating and how this affected what was written by men. We also gave an outline of some 'female perspectives' on what we perceived to be male ideas. We asked further questions to be pursued, hopefully by women, many of which we also continue to consider.

This writing on gender was put aside while we decided to 'put our female money where our female mouths were' and write a book about play and playwork – *Reflective Playwork* (2010) – which has been successfully published and received. We are now working on a second edition. During this time, however, we continued to pursue our work on the female perspective which developed into a much wider field of research around children's development of gender roles and sexuality and its relationship to play, playwork and other provision for children, including the role of people who work or live with children. We have presented various aspects of this at conferences together – alone and with others – and since the publication of our first book, we have presented an academic paper to the International Play Association which brought together different aspects of our thinking that we hope to crystallize within this book.

We have come a long way since 2006. Much of which we wrote about in our early chapters now seems ill considered. Some is still relevant, but we were too quick to believe many of the theories that we read about the differences between males and females, before we had considered all the opposing views. We are no more certain now than we were previously about the foundations of gender and sexuality, but we are more knowledgeable about the research that has been carried out and the range of ideas that abound in relation to it and we still have many questions.

Since deciding to write this book we have been pondering on our own gendered pasts. Why are we bothered about sex and gender in relation to children's play? Perhaps writing this book will solve this question or perhaps it will pose further ones – for both us and our readers.

We believe it is very difficult to disassociate ourselves from whom we have become. We believe that who we have been or we are at any one time in our lives is part of our past, our present and our expectations of a future and we don't feel that we have been the same throughout it all. How much is uniquely us, genetically modified us, socialized us, gendered us, aging us or expected us, is beyond us! However, in order to acknowledge our own history, we follow with a short account of some aspects of our own gendering.

Jacky

I was born on 6 January, Jacqueline, daughter to Cliff and Gwen, younger sister to Judy – thus I was labelled as female from birth – a girl, with a girl's name, daughter and sister, with a father and mother. I was born into a 'gendered' world! If I had not been labelled as a female from birth, would I have grown up in another way?

I was brought up in a female dominated household – my father worked nights, he just earned the money and bought us treats, but the seat of power rested very heavily with my grandmother, mother and aunties. My playmates were all girls – girl cousins, girl friends and girl enemies – boys were really an irrelevance, apart from the occasional annoyance of one boy cousin who tried to join in and one boy neighbour who tried to give me and two friends a bit of early sex education – boys did not feature. I had no thought or concern at that time, as to whether what I was playing or who I was playing with was 'girly' or not. Did my playing influence who I am? I am trying to work that out, as it is relevant to the basis of this book.

I played a lot of make believe games – horses, mums and dads, home, school and hospitals. I read, wrote stories, drew pictures, made up codes, played outside with water, mud, sticks and stones and small creatures; climbed trees; rode my bike; played catch, hide and seek, sardines, hopscotch, ball, hula hoop, rounders and French cricket; walked on stilts, jumped on and off high things; swung and danced; I did French knitting, Scooby doo and made dens, formed secret clubs; dreamed and on and on. Life was play. Would my play life have been the same if I had not been labelled a 'girl'? I think not.

I went to an all girls school and there I made more girl friends and girl enemies until my girl friends and I started being interested in boys – to begin with, in a 'virtual' sort of way, through gossip from more 'experienced' girls and then in a different way. Boys were an unknown quantity. I was very shy with them (actually I was generally shy with everyone), but I covered this up by appearing 'cool'. I fancied boys from afar and dressed in a way that I hoped attracted them and then didn't know how to behave when I did. Would I have been like this if I had not been labelled a 'girl'? I started my periods – a messy affair – that I dreaded each month until I became accustomed to the associated paraphernalia, feelings of discomfort and concern that were a part of it. Did I become more female because of this biological milestone – the joining of the 'club' for women only? Certainly, no man can possibly understand how it feels to menstruate; how the emotions are stirred, how the body and mind respond – but I am sure they, too, have their own biological milestones to experience. Are these biological processes linked to our gendered behaviour or is gender a socialized aspect of our being? Perhaps writing this book will help with this question? It is strange to think that maybe I am a construct!

Ali

I have always been interested in the gender dance. I use the word 'dance' because this word does seem to describe it; sometimes the steps seem to be carved out already, sometimes there are new ones to create, sometimes it involves a partner or a group and at other times it's a tentative or a triumphant solo. But this dance never ends; it is always evolving and changing and it refuses to be pinned down and given a name, definite music and set rhythms and that's why I continue to be fascinated by it. It is certainly bigger than we are.

My dance began as a child – I was born in the fifties, when expectations for girls and boys were very different, but I had a great role model in my mother who was one of the only working mothers I knew. I had two older brothers so it went without saying that I was a 'tomboy' (although I don't like that word – it's another stereotypical label that doesn't fit). I refused to fit neatly into the 'girl' box, but leapt in and out of it throughout childhood, playing with the boys one day and dominating my younger sisters the next, exploring feelings and trying on identities as if they were sets of costumes. I climbed on roofs and trees, cliffs and rocks, explored building sites and woods, played football and cricket and plenty of pirates, cowboys and Indians, cops and robbers and tracking etc. But I also played schools and gymnastic displays with my sisters (guess who took the lead roles), had a late 'doll phase' and got briefly immersed in creating Sindy families and homes at a friend's house. In the school playground, I alternated between racing the boys and skipping with the girls and had a great time playing kiss chase. I also spent hours and hours reading and writing poems and stories and thinking about life and death and the point of everything and I still do.

Puberty changed the dance entirely – I could no longer pretend I was a boy and so had to find out what it meant to be a woman in a world that, although changing, still favoured men. Becoming a mother – and a wife – changed the dance again and I both learnt and choreographed some whole new routines including those for stepmother and foster mother and these too continue to flicker and to flourish at different times. Is fatherhood different to motherhood? That's a complex ballet ... And while I have far less angst about all this these days and there are far more tunes to step out to, I am still dancing, still twirling along the continuum of refusing to be defined and looking for definitions.

I have concluded one thing – although if experience is anything to go by, this may change – that gender and sexuality are two colourful and often colliding spectrums that we all dance along and even though we sometimes long to stop, claim the spotlight on the dance floor and sing out 'this is me', we will find we will soon be moving away again as the set or the music changes.

While I have had times when I have been proud to be a woman, these are more like verses in my life-song where the underlying and repeated refrain for me is 'can't we all just be human?'

The following chapters explore notions about the nature of gender, sex and children's play and how these inform each other. Our own histories may well be reflected in the real-life examples we will also share. But here's a thought to begin with. Hughes (2012) suggests that play has a genetic component – what we see when children are playing may be partially acquired, but the basis for the play behaviour has been stored and passed on genetically through successive generations since the time that it originally evolved to aid survival. Might this also be true of our gendered and sexualized behaviour? What is biologically determined and what is socially constructed? Read on.

INTRODUCTION

If you have read the Preface you will have read a little about our gendered paths and we hope that this will stir your thoughts about your own gendered childhood, and equally how this may affect you and your role in relation to children and young people and their gendered present and future. It is only through reflection such as this that we can truly put our own behaviour into the context of the here and now. We hope this book will act as a catalyst for you doing just that.

The chapters will stand alone, but in order to see how gender, sex and play are intimately related to each other and the lives of children, you will need to give each one your consideration. We have included a glossary, as you may find some of the terms used are unfamiliar. Please also note that we intentionally do not use 'he' or 'she' or 'his' or 'her' in the book, unless referring to a specific child. We use 'they and 'their', instead, which, although not grammatically correct, represent a non-gendered way of talking about a child.

Chapter 1 gives us an introduction to the enquiry in the book and to the multifaceted construct called 'play', giving an outline of its characteristics and some of the many reasons that are given for why children do play. The chapter gives real life examples of gender and sexuality in action during play and finally outlines meanings of some of the words and how we intend to use them in the book.

Chapter 2 looks at the history of, and reasons for, the interest in there being potential differences in the ways that boys and girls play. It explores notions of patriarchy, feminism, femininity, masculinity and children's play from the recent past and then considers whether current childhood is being sexualized. The chapter also considers whether the development of boys and girls is affected if they play differently.

Chapter 3 examines published research on where differences have been seen in the play of boys and girls and then compares it with recent observational and anecdotal examples, which are divided into: play styles, physical play; themes for pretend play; activities and interests; groups and, finally, friendships. The chapter considers why boys and girls may appear to play differently and whether gendered toys play a part in these potential differences.

Chapter 4 analyses the theories that abound which try to explain what causes potential differences between males and females with particular reference to children and their play. This chapter outlines the disciplines from which the researchers come and what might motivate them to carry out research that considers whether there are, or are not, differences between males and females. The ethics of research with children is explored.

Chapter 5 is about children's sexuality and their sexual play. It challenges us with some exploratory questions, which are answered at the end and then explains why sexual play has become a matter of concern for playworkers. The chapter provides expert opinion on children's under-standing of sexuality and considers the problems that some adults have with this. It also looks briefly at intersex and the genderization and sexualization of our society and the problems that these issues can cause to children.

Chapter 6 considers the role of adults who work with children and their views on children's gendered and sexual play. It further looks at how much influence adults might have over children's expression of gender and sexuality and outlines various ways that adults intervene in relation to children and gender and considers adults' reactions to children's play of a sexual nature.

The final chapter, Chapter 7, looks at what might be considered 'normative' sexual behaviour between birth and puberty and when behaviour may give cause for concern. It looks at the notion of 'healthy' gender play and looking back over the concerns that have been raised throughout the book suggests that play deprivation and play bias might be more appropriate areas of concern. The chapter introduces the notion of becoming consciously competent in relation to gender and sex in children's play and finally reprises three categories of thought related to its themes and re-emphasizes why play is equally important for boys and girls.

CHAPTER ONE

Gender and sex: The play perspective

Introduction

Why a book on sex, gender and play? As many authors have said, we never set out to write such a book; it evolved naturally from our interest, our experience and our moment in history. We have always been fascinated with and by playing and playwork has become central to our working lives. But we have also lived through a half-century that has seen more societal and attitudinal change to gender and sexuality than any other. These huge shifts in thinking and behaving have played out through us – our own lives have been greatly affected by the various waves of feminism and campaigns for equality and our own views and queries on gender particularly, have catapulted backwards and forwards over the decades and are still not fixed. Our society is riddled with the effects of this and many people have strong opinions on how gender and sexuality influences and shapes human beings. Fine (2011: 3) gives a wonderful illustration of this.

> Suppose a researcher were to tap you on the shoulder and ask you to write down what, according to cultural lore, males and females are like. Would you stare at the researcher blankly and exclaim 'But what can you mean? Every person is a unique, multifaceted, sometimes even contradictory individual, and with such an astonishing range of personality traits within each sex, and across contexts, social class, age, experience, educational level, sexuality and ethnicity, it would be pointless and meaningless to attempt to pigeonhole such rich complexity and variability into two crude stereotypes'? No. You'd pick up your pencil and start writing.

We believe an open mind is essential to embarking on these three very complicated, unsolved and interrelated subjects of gender, sex and play. We have trawled a great deal of literature from all sides of the ongoing arguments on these topics. Many authors believe that they are not only right, but also condemn other perspectives: this has caused us to regularly debate with each other and to question where and why we find bias in ourselves and in others. We feel this kind of open fluidity is fundamental to genuine enquiry, although it certainly takes practice and commitment (and tests the co-author relationship!), but it also brings some relief that there are no necessarily right answers to find and champion – as Nouwen (1976: 77) has recognized:

> Frequently we are restlessly looking for answers, going from door to door, from book to book, or from school to school, without having really listened carefully and attentively to the questions. Rilke says to the young poet:
> 'Do not now seek answers which cannot be given you because you would not be able to live them. And the point is to live everything. *Live* the questions now. Perhaps you will then gradually, without noticing it, live along some distant day into the answer.'

So, there you have it. This is not a book that gives answers – it is a book that asks questions and tests and scrutinizes answers. We will explore the thoughts of those who have tried to answer them from a range of different perspectives. We have formed and reformed our opinions, but we have found it difficult to come to definitive conclusions. We have, however, fashioned different questions and we do offer some thoughts for better practice – and so we invite you to join our quest. To do this, you will also need to recognize – as we have had to do – that none of us 'see things as they are. We see things as *we* are' (Nin 1961: 124).

Areas of interest

We are interested in:

- the everyday experiences of boys and girls, whether there are differences and what might be the cause of these;
- how children play in response to these possible differences;
- whether children's play culture impacts on their current and future lives; and
- whether adult responses to children playing help or hinder children and society.

In this chapter, we will first look at the subject of play in children's lives, as this is the foundation of our thinking. We will look at definitions and claims made for the benefits of playing. We will then go on to clarify what we mean by certain terminology and how words and concepts like sex,

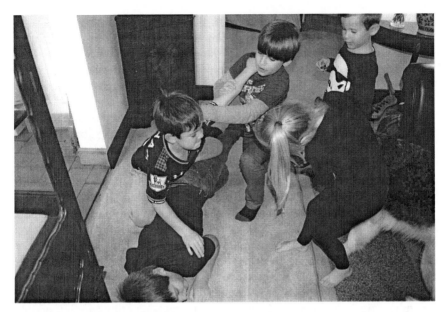

FIGURE 1.1 *Here's to play*
Permission granted by Statham and Statham

sexuality and gender are used and misused and indeed how these concepts are played with throughout childhood, for like all children's thoughts and experiences, they are expressed in their playing.

What is play?

In current Western society, we do not appear to see the world through children's eyes and we are not well acquainted with the 'life-force' that is play. Many of us tend to see play as almost optional for children when there is nothing more constructive to do – at its best it keeps children occupied while we are busy with the real stuff of life; at its worst it seems to blend many 'unpleasant' behaviours with noise, chaos and mess. But this shows just how deeply we have lost touch with the essence of play for us humans – how fundamental it is for our past, present and future and particularly how much it matters to children.

In 2013, the United Nations produced a General Comment to urge the world to take seriously the 'forgotten' Article 31 in the Convention on the Rights of the Child and to guide the governments of the then 194 countries who had ratified the Convention to actively promote societal attitudes that support and encourage the creation of time and space for children to engage in spontaneous play, recreation and creativity. How timely this is, although also sad, that it has become necessary to remind the world not to erode children's natural and essential drive to play. Let us set out our stall here. We believe with Brown that 'play seems so important to our development and survival that the impulse to play has become a biological drive. Like our desires for food, sleep or sex, the impulse to play is internally generated' (2009: 42). As Groos (1901: 369) stated over a century ago – 'for a series of years we find life virtually controlled by play. Before systematic education begins, the child's whole existence, except the time devoted to sleeping and eating, is occupied with play, which thus becomes the single, absorbing aim of his life'. Play is something that human beings and many other animals simply and instinctively do, as often as they possibly can and especially – but not exclusively – while growing up. We believe with others Smith (2010), Bjorkland (2007), Sutton-Smith (1997), Beckoff and Byers (1998), Hughes (2012), that it is biologically essential and so commands our respect and interest.

Much has been written about play by a variety of people, from a range of different fields, attempting to define and explain it. In the last few decades there seems to be scholarly agreement that play is so wide-ranging in its' manifestations, so complex in its integration of brain, body and emotions, so ambiguous in its' perceived benefits, that 'true' definitions are impossible and elusive. There are:

> a number of conceptual and methodological problems associated with attempts to establish the benefits of play outside of a deprivation model. These are the difficulties of defining 'play' in a variety of social and spatial contexts; the complex models required to examine causal relationships; the difficulties inherent in longitudinal studies without clear control groups; and changes in the definitions and functions of 'play' as young people develop. (Beunderman 2010: 4)

Nevertheless, there is some agreement about certain characteristics of playing – Ellis (1973), Garvey (1977), Lester and Russell (2008), Bateson (1955), Caillois (2001), Burghardt (2005), Hughes (2001), Bruner (1983), Brown (2009), Huizinga (1955), Lillemyr (2009), Pellegrini (2009), Smith (2010), Sutton-Smith (1997) and Else (2014) – that is, what seems to hold true regardless of the behaviour or context, or as Millar (1968: 21) puts it:

> Perhaps play is best used as an adverb; not as a name of a class of activities, nor as distinguished by the accompanying mood, but to describe how and under what conditions an action is performed.

These characteristics suggest that whatever a child is doing – whether they are running about chasing, talking to themselves while moving around or sitting on the ground exploring an object, we can consider it likely that the child is actually playing if the following are present:

- Voluntary, chosen – children cannot be forced to play or directed to do so, it is their free choice. They 'cannot be passive recipients of play and that since they are actively involved, this encourages autonomous thinking' (Rogers and Sawyer [1988] in Cole-Hamilton et al. 2002: 15).

- Intrinsically motivated – children cannot be bribed into playing – play is instinctively performed for no external goal or reward. Hughes (2001: 1) describes play as the 'behavioural and psychic equivalent of oxygen'.

- Done for its own sake – play is often described as a process that doesn't depend on any outcomes or products (although these often follow). 'It is characterized by "means rather than end" – the process of the play is more important than any end point or goal that is obvious to participant or the naïve onlooker' (Smith, 2005: 271).

- Flexible – children, when playing, try out many and diverse kinds of language, objects, actions, attitudes, atmospheres – and the more stimulating and varied the environment there is, the more possibilities for a range of responses. They change tack, test this and try that, wreck their creations and often never do what they set out to do, because play 'provides an excellent opportunity to try combinations of behaviour that would, under functional pressure, never be tried' (Bruner 1972: 38).

- Unpredictable, uncertain – children often seek out opportunities to take risks, respond to dares, indulge in the forbidden, suggesting that 'children's play provides a primary behaviour for developing resilience [...] an ability that allows individuals to overcome or resist severe risks or chronic stress factors in the environment' (Lester and Russell 2008: 47).

- Pleasurable, enjoyable – anyone observing children playing can see this – an obviously 'enjoyable and largely harmless activity (that) is something to be treasured and celebrated' (Smith 2010: 216).

- Spontaneous and timeless – children playing are 'fully in the moment, in the zone and lose a sense of the passage of time' (Brown 2009: 17). Hughes (2002: 24) describes children playing as being 'immersed' – 'being engaged in a play experience with such focus and intensity, that temporary sensory dissociation from external reality occurs'.

- Non-literal, 'as-if', simulated behaviour that imitates reality but also clearly indicates to other players that this is 'not-real', this is 'pretend'. Lester and Russell (2010: 8) describe this as a playful disposition – 'a belief in being able to change and have control over external conditions'.

But is there a point to children's play; does it have purpose? There are many theories but they fall into two main schools of thought; that of deferred or present benefits. The first states that play is necessary for our all-round development, i.e. playing helps us become better adults. The second states that play is necessary for a good childhood, i.e. playing enriches children's lives in the here-and-now. Both of course can be true – Brown (2014: 12–14) skilfully and usefully brings both process and product together, but the former paradigm has tended to dominate thinking, obscuring both the natural courses of growth and the rich spontaneous reality of play and thereby excusing all kinds of adult intervention and control to 'make play happen' or to channel play in a specific direction.

In their Playwork Principles (see Appendix A), the playwork sector in the UK makes statements about play in the first two principles; namely,

1   All children and young people need to play. The impulse to play is innate. Play is a biological, psychological and social necessity, and is fundamental to the healthy development and well being of individuals and communities.

2   Play is a process that is freely chosen, personally directed and intrinsically motivated. That is, children and young people determine and control the content and intent of their play, by following their own instincts, ideas and interests, in their own way for their own reasons.

These statements have been widely quoted and debated and are still in use, although many in the playwork sector now feel they are insufficient and a little clumsy; Brown (2014: 17) gives a good critique that examines how many forms of play can be 'chosen', but not 'freely', 'directed' but not 'personally', 'motivated' but not 'intrinsically'. The Playwork Principles have been useful though in describing play as being children's domain and not something that adults should lead, direct or organize – a much needed concept in a society that has become less and less tolerant of children's play.

Gaskins et al. (2007) describe three kinds of society and their attitudes to play – 'culturally cultivated play', 'culturally accepted play' and 'culturally curtailed play' and it is, indeed, remarkable to see how, on the whole, the UK has moved *in just half a century* from the second (where adults expect children to play and accept this, but don't particularly get involved) towards the third kind of society (where play is not seen as especially purposeful, but a useful distraction to occasionally occupy children when adults see fit). Many professionals within the children's workforce also espouse the first attitude (where play is used as a vehicle for educating children and promoting values).

The importance of play

Play seems to be necessary for a whole contested variety of reasons and we will explore some of these briefly.

Species survival

Much research has been done on animal play and attempts made to explain why play behaviour evolved. Spinka et al. (2001) hypothesize that play is 'training for the unexpected' and equips animals to be more flexible and successful in their responses to potential and actual threats. This idea is supported by other ethologists, ecologists and primatologists Burghardt (2005), Bekoff (2007), Goodall (1990) and taken up by anthropologists and psychologists Bateson (1955), Fagen (1981), Kalliala (2006) and Brown (2009), to indicate that play does seem to be an adaptive behaviour. Smith (2005: 271) comments:

> The ubiquity of forms of play throughout most mammal species and humans in all cultures studied to date, and the time, energy and sometimes danger costs of engaging in them, strongly suggest that selective pressures have acted to favour play behaviours and that they have some functional value for the player, even if he or she is not fully aware of it. However, the range of functions for play and strength of evidence for them is still a matter of considerable debate.

Physical development

Children have a natural urge to run, jump, climb and spin and this is regularly expressed in their playing. Groos (1901: 83) famously linked physical development with play as the natural means by which children grow and gain control over their muscles:

> Almost as soon as the child has learned to preserve his equilibrium in ordinary walking, he proceeds to complicate the problem by trying to walk on kerbstones, in a rut, on a beam, on a balustrade or narrow wall.

It is clear that vigorous playful movement enhances muscle growth and healthy cardiovascular development and more notably at present, combats obesity.

Several schools that have recently installed Scrapstore Playpods in their playgrounds have noted that within just a few weeks, their teachers are seeing greater physical competencies in the majority of children in physical education lessons. The children had been having such fun roaring around the playground using pieces of scrap in diverse ways, that they had naturally improved their hand-eye coordination, their balance, their spatial awareness and their stamina levels.

Emotional regulation and resilience

Playing builds emotional strength and adaptability and nurtures self-control through allowing experience of strong emotions while composing and then imposing game rules and rituals. Themes of violence, death, bodily functions, loss and tragedy are common in play, but all those playing know this is 'not real' and so they can experiment with 'possible feelings and possible identities without risking the real biological or social consequences' (Bailey, 2002: 171). A number of scholars and scientists Sutton-Smith (2003), Panksepp (2007), Gayler and Evans (2001), Else (2014) have in recent years been exploring the role of play in both expression and control of primary emotions like anger, fear, sadness and disgust and conclude that these playful experiences significantly contribute to emotional control and stability in everyday 'real' life.

Brain growth

Neuroscience has advanced our understanding of brain development and as technology increases, more will no doubt be discovered about this amazing organ. As with all research questions and methods however, these do need to be objectively selected and interpretations of findings done with great care, as there have been many conclusions made and publicized to date that have been later unsupported or discredited. However, the current accepted wisdom is that the brain grows and develops and changes throughout life in response to mind and body experience and that this is particularly true of childhood – billions of synaptic connections are made in our early years to promote brain function during this time. Animal studies have shown that the wide-ranging, flexible nature of playing seems to optimize neural growth and integrate brain systems and indicate that play is vital for maintaining plasticity. Experiments depriving rats of play (Pellis and Pellis, 2007) have resulted in frontal lobe damage and huge social stress. As 'each animal's brain enables it to live in its own world' (Lester and Russell 2008: 44) we cannot automatically assume that other animals – and humans – would experience the same effects, but there is certainly plenty to indicate play may be pivotal to brain development.

Intellectual advancement

Play aids learning and provokes experimentation and exploration to find factual answers. Children are naturally curious and explore and discover – they want to know why things are as they are and will pursue knowledge when something has sufficiently grabbed their attention (even though that something may seem insignificant to us). Play has been considered to be such a powerful process in promoting learning that we have tried to incorporate playing into our educational methods although this has often backfired when we retain control and try to make play happen. As Elkind (2007: 128) says, 'self-directed play experiences nourish and support the child's maturing mental abilities'.

Spiritual experience

Children ponder and explore questions about life, birth, death, the earth and the universe in their play. They relish time outside to experience nature first-hand and have endless curiosity about their place in the time-space continuum, beginnings and endings and all things 'supernatural'. This evokes a deep sense of wonder which is,

> first of all, a response to the novelty of experience. Wonder is itself a kind of expectancy of fulfilment. The child's sense of wonder, displayed as surprise and joy, is aroused as a response to the mystery of some external stimulus that promises 'more to come' or better still 'more to do' – the power of perceptual participation in the known and the unknown. (Cobb 1977: 28)

Arousal

Play stimulates and, therefore, helps in maintaining an optimal level in the central nervous system and keeping it balanced, seeking out new and/ or wild experiences right through to seeking out calm and self-nurturing experiences. Gayler and Evans (2001) talk about play maintaining a level of arousal that is both tolerable and flexible enough to support adaptive behaviour.

Social competence

While children can and do play alone, they also seek out other children to play with. Some adults lazily assume that children are mostly competitive and likely to fall out and need early adult intervention. However, genuine and un-hasty observation of children playing usually reveals plenty of conflict but also a great deal of negotiation, compromise and under-standing. Gray (2013: 34) states:

FIGURE 1.2 *Shall we do it this way?*
Permission granted by Statham, Cid-Garcia and Brillot

Play is not something one has to do; players are always free to quit. In social play, each player knows that anyone who feels unhappy will quit, and if too many quit, the game ends. To keep the game going, players must satisfy not only their own desires but also those of the other players. The intense drive that children have to play with other children, therefore, is a powerful force for them to learn how to attend to others' wishes and negotiate differences.

Life satisfaction

'The process of playing gives the glorious sensation of a stronger sense of self. Play can be deeply satisfying.' (McMahon 2009: 6). This alone makes an argument for play viable – all children deserve a childhood filled with memories of playing. 'Is it any wonder that often the times we feel most alive, those that make up our best memories, are moments of play?' (Brown 2009: 5).

Creative appreciation

Play fosters imaginative invention and problem solving through make-believe and symbolism. 'Wherever playfulness prevails, there is always a surprising element, surpassing mere repetition or habituation' (Erikson 1977: 17). Newson and Newson (1979: 12) describe how it is the 'supreme flexibility' in play that makes it 'the ideal setting or jumping-off point for creative thinking and imaginative invention'. Children often come up with amazing ideas and inventions when playing as they are not restricted by notions of how things ought to be.

Identity formation

Children explore and try out roles when playing – roles of people they know or media characters – and often do so to also test others' responses. It could be argued that this is all part of forming their own personal and social identity – 'who am I? Who are you? Who are we? What are all the possibilities and where do these, start and stop?' 'Play under the control of the player gives to the child his first and the most crucial opportunity to have the courage to think, to talk and perhaps even to be himself' (Bruner 1983: 69). Being a child is also for children an identity in itself and is really important to children who 'always seek to have their own separate play culture' (Sutton-Smith 1997: 125) and delight in covert teasing and joking about adults. As we will go on to see, children also explore and test out their gender and sexual identities too when playing.

Trauma resolution

Children use play as a way to discharge their feelings, work out their fears, make sense of their worries, and to replay and come to terms with traumatic life events. 'To play it out is the most natural self-healing method childhood affords' (Erikson 1965: 215). For most children, this happens without adults even knowing – being able to discharge anger by furiously kicking an object around or re-enact fear by putting a toy animal in a perilous situation helps them to gain mastery of their feelings without hurting anyone else. Sometimes children with real distress in their lives can also benefit from time with a play therapist who will allow them to lead the play and trust they will know what to do to heal themselves (Chown 2014).

Empathic emergence

To play with someone else entails initially recognizing their play signals and then their intentions – quite possibly the bedrock of empathy. Much has been written about the social value of 'pretend play'. 'Using imagination enables children to plan actions, anticipate their own and other people's behaviour and to empathize with others' (Lester and Russell 2008: 56).

Stress management

'Real play springs from within us and one of its many properties is to help us deal with stress' (Crowe 1983: 2). Having time and space to play where we are in control is a great leveller and helps us – both adults and children – relax. However, it is interesting to note that children also introduce low-level stresses into their games and put themselves into situations that are stressful. Rutter (2006) argues that some kinds of stress are positive and help us develop better ways of coping and responding to present and future life events. Some moderate external and environmental challenges also promote greater physical and emotional health (Yun et al. 2005). Play mixes reality and unreality and offers opportunities for active control and mastery and the urge to play in children seems to take account of this.

Language construction

Children appropriate and use language all the time in their playing and in fact play with language itself – 'they reverse words, they rhyme, they play with alliterative and onomatopoeic sounds and they create the most wonderful nonsense verse' (Jenkinson 2001: 87). They naturally name what they see and experience and the high levels of symbolism in their playing are the precursors and foundation of language, which after all is in itself symbolic.

Sensory evolvement

'Children's senses cry out to be used first to provide the experiences that they will later need in order to connect. Children must feel the world, listen to it, see it, taste it, smell it, know it and us. That takes time and a great deal of silent investigation in peace and privacy' (Crowe 1983: 39). Playing is often a highly sensory experience, especially outdoors (Chown 2014).

Induce further playing

'Successful play experience increases the potential for continued happy playing' (Sutton-Smith 1997: 44). Children would play from dawn to dusk if allowed so to do for as far as they are concerned, the benefits they obviously derive from playing drive them to keep doing so.

Play – in all its manifestations – is indeed an important behaviour and particularly so for children. While it is impossible to prove the above claims and unattainable to pin down what playing really is, we would do well to observe it with renewed respect, remembering that:

> When we watch a child play, we only see a small part of what is going on. Children play with their whole selves: It is a somatic, sensual, emotional, cognitive, social and spiritual phenomenon. All we see is the external manifestation. (Russell 2005: 104)

Observing children playing can nevertheless be enlightening and will certainly generate many questions in the objective observer! We cannot be certain what children are thinking and feeling when playing, so many questions must remain unanswered, but if we remain open-minded and non-judgemental we may still discover that children's play cultures are broader and deeper than we first thought.

Thus, we come to relating play to our other subjects – gender and sexuality. We give below some anecdotal examples.

Examples

- A four-year-old boy returns from his first day at school saying sorrowfully but firmly that pink can no longer be his favourite colour and he will need a different coloured lunchbox tomorrow.

- Several eight-year-old girls are building a 'hotel' with cargo nets around a wooden pagoda in a junior school playground and create a 'reception area' complete with an old phone, keyboards and carpet tiles. Three boys of similar age come to 'raid' as they did yesterday, but the girls are ready for them and say they need them to act as bodyguards and stop anyone else 'taking our stuff'. The boys immediately take to this new role and take up cardboard tubes as 'weapons' and stand on guard ready to repel all boarders, while the girls happily continue.

- 'Boys stink!' shout the girls from their den. 'Girls are rubbish!' shout back the boys from theirs.

- 'He must be gay if he likes to play with girls,' says a six-year-old boy to his friend observing another boy dressing up.

- A five-year-old boy and girl are heard giggling inside a cardboard structure. A ten-year-old boy is heard telling another boy 'leave them alone, they're shagging'.

- Two five-year-old girls are discussing clothes for their dolls. 'They need padded bras to look right,' says one. 'Yeah, and shorts and high heels' says the other.

- A six-year-old boy was playing with cars in the sandpit at his after-school club, making runways etc. Then, oblivious of everyone, he took off all his clothes and sat in the sand, quietly pouring it over himself and murmuring to himself.

- Two ten-year-old girls are making bangles and chatting – their whole conversation is about who they are going out with (although in reality neither is going out with anyone) and how their 'boyfriends' like them to be.

All of these are real-life, every day happenings we have observed ourselves or been told about by colleagues – we have collected many such stories.

Reflective questions

What is going on in all these snapshots of children playing? Is there anything to concern us? Should an adult intervene in any way, and if so, why and how? Or is this all quite 'normal'?

Whatever our response to these questions and whether we like it or not, it is clear that children themselves are affected by and playing with the concepts of gender and sexuality and we will go on to explore many such examples in Chapters 3, 5 and 6.

Definitions

First, we need to clarify what we mean by certain words and how we will be using them in this book, as some other researchers/authors use these words in different ways or use different words to mean the same thing.

Sex

We use the word 'sex' in two ways. First of all, by sex we mean the biological, genetic differences that are observed at birth. With some notable exceptions, females are born with vaginas, ovaries filled with eggs, wombs and the potential to grow breasts, menstruate and have babies. They have some different hormones to males – most notably oestrogen and progesterone. Males are born with a penis that has the potential to become erect, testicles with sperm that can be ejaculated from the penis, the potential to father babies and, with some exceptions, they have more testosterone than females. Second of all, we use the word 'sex' in relation to sexual experience, arousal and action.

Intersex

The 'exceptions' in the preceding paragraph include those people described as 'intersex' because they are born with a reproductive or sexual anatomy that doesn't seem to fit the typical definitions of male or female as described above. We explore this further in Chapter 5, but statistical estimates seem to indicate that intersex people may be as common as people with red hair. As often happens in biological science, it is by studying intersex people and their differences and life experiences, that we gain a greater understanding of the whole and recognize that a simple bipolar approach – you're either male or female – is crude and definitely exclusive.

Gender

We use the word gender to describe our awareness and reaction to our assigned biological sex, which is influenced by biological, psychological and social factors. Are you a girl or a boy baby? Will you grow into a man or a woman? By the age of about two years most children have a notion of whether they are a boy or a girl and they gradually grow more aware of the biological differences between males and females.

Gender Identity

Awareness of physical differences develops into a private experience of feeling like a male or a female – our gender identity. Generally, but not always, a person's gender identity is in line with their biological sex. Intersex people too, adopt a gender identity of being a man or a woman. However, Dr Robin Dea, a mental health specialist comments 'we feel our gender identity in our soul, but it is on a continuum and it can evolve' (Dea, in Pfaff 2011: 193), illustrating the complexities of identity formation and the ongoing and interweaving effects and influences of genes, hormones, societal expectations, life experiences and the environment.

Gender role

Gender role is the public expression of gender; it is ways of being and behaving that are considered to be masculine, feminine or somewhere in between. This being and behaviour are both influenced by experience and biology, but the extent to which one has the greater influence than the other, is a point of considerable and ongoing contention within the scientific world and for many others, some of whom consider that people can be severely disadvantaged by the gender role that they play out in society. Gender roles are variable depending on context and external feedback, particularly in modern societies. Usually – but not always – a person's gender identity corresponds with *their* gender role (using 'his' or 'her' denotes an acceptance of a binary model of gender and we are specifically questioning that here and in other parts of the book). We also use the words 'gendered' and 'genderized'.

Gendered

This term – first coined in 1972 – is an adjective applied to a person, object, action or saying, which has been considered to be either male or female or significantly biased towards one sex or the other.

Genderized

To genderize is a verb and it is the act of making or judging something to be 'gendered', i.e. we may divide or categorize on the basis of gender distinctions or we may assign gender identity in regard to social or cultural differences.

Sexuality

Sexuality is the capacity for sexual feeling and arousal or a person's sexual preferences for particular types of activity that arouse them.

> Although each child comes to form his or her sexuality in a unique way, there are patterns of sexuality formation common for both boys and girls. At an early age, children begin to form an understanding of the ways that bodies look and function for both sexes, often through a process of body discovery in which children become aware of their bodies as part of themselves and part of their identity. (Schuhrke 2000: 1537)

Gender does not necessarily denote sexuality. Sexuality is also a term sometimes used to question whether a person is homosexual, bisexual, heterosexual or somewhere on that spectrum.

Adults can have difficulty with children's emerging sexuality because they view it through an adult lens rather than seeing that children are playfully exploring bodies and terminology in order to gradually understand what sex and sexuality is. The way that adults impart information and respond to children's sexual play, can have a profound effect on how comfortable children become with their later sexual behaviour and sexual identity – but we will explore all this and more in Chapter 5.

We have looked at definitions and meanings of our three subjects – sex, gender and play. We now go on to look at how these interrelate in both the past and the present and in children's lives. Preves (2005: 2) comments that 'sex and gender operate as inflexible and central organizing principles of daily existence'. How has that affected all of us and more importantly, how does this influence children and their play?

Suggested reading

Brown, F. (2014), *Play & Playwork 101 Stories of Children Playing*, Maidenhead: Open University Press.

Lester, S. and W. Russell (2008), *Play for a Change*, London: National Children's Bureau.

Lester, S. and W. Russell (2010), *Children's Right to Play: An Examination of the Importance of Play in the Lives of Children Worldwide*, Working Paper No. 57. The Hague, The Netherlands: Bernard van Leer Foundation.

CHAPTER TWO

Gender and sexuality in childhood – perspectives past and present

Introduction

In this chapter we briefly explore the history of interest in gender and sexuality and how this influences children. In the introduction to her book, *Delusions of Gender*, Fine (2011: xxviii) says:

> It's worth remembering just how much society can change in a relatively short period of time. Precedents are still being set. Could a society in which males and females hold equal places ever exist? No one knows whether males and females could ever enjoy perfect equality.

Equality is not about being the same. It is about equal rights and opportunities; but no one knows whether this is what society as a whole wants. No one knows exactly what this equality would be. In the history of our society, issues of equality are mainly recent phenomena and ones that are still largely unresolved. We think that some of the precedents of which Fine speaks are actually being reversed.

Reflective question

Can you think of changes, related to gender and sexuality that have happened during your lifetime?

This chapter will look at why in recent times it has become a matter of importance for society to consider issues related to gender and sexuality in childhood. What part does children's play feature in the ongoing struggle to make sense of possible equality of opportunity for males and females and people of different sexual persuasions? In pursuit of this, does it matter if boys and girls play in a stereotypically male or female way?

Patriarchy

This current interest in gender and sexuality comes at the end of a long run of 'men in charge' – patriarchal societies where women have played a subordinate role. Some anthropological studies tend to suggest that men and women were far more equal in ancient times. There are certainly many who believe that early civilizations existed that were matriarchal. But no anthropologists or archaeologists, feminists included, appear to have found evidence of such societies. 'The search for a genuinely egalitarian, let alone matriarchal, culture has proved fruitless,' concludes Ortner (1974: 24). However the business of looking at history with a gender-sensitive eye is in its infancy. In his article on patriarchy, Zerzan (n.d.) suggests that there was a long span of time when women were generally less subject to men, before male-defined culture became fixed or universal. There are many theories about the origins of patriarchy. For instance, Rubin (1979: 176) concludes that the 'world-historical defeat of women occurred with the origins of culture and is a prerequisite of culture.' Her idea suggests that when humans were foragers and hunter-gatherers, the responsibility for providing food and caring for children, was shared equally between men and women as a group. However, with the advent of so-called 'civilization' isolated and privatized family life became the norm and the concept of 'the family' with all its inequalities was born. 'Mothering' and nurturing became the female role and providing food and protection the male role and over time this male role somehow assumed greater importance. Another idea is that patriarchy was born as a consequence of human reproduction. Life was short, so women had to have many children and thus their time was taken up constantly with giving birth and looking after babies with little time for other non-domestic tasks.

There are some who suggest that there are no anthropological records showing even equality between the sexes. They believe that anthropological records show that all societies have been patriarchies. Sociologist Steven Goldberg (2004) suggests that all past societies have been dominated by men and that this is an inevitable resolution of the psycho-physiological reality. Anthropologist Marvin Harris (1977) suggested somewhat bizarrely that because men are mostly stronger than women, they became the warriors and women were the enticement or reward for men risking their lives in battle. Whatever the view point, it is certain that in most, if not all past cultures, men have been dominant. As Ortner (1974: 87) suggests in her polemic 'Is female to male as nature is to culture?':

[T]he implications for social change are circular – a different cultural view can only grow out of a different social actuality and a different social actuality can only grow out of a different cultural view.

Feminism has sought to develop this different cultural view and, over time, this has had an effect on the way that some people view the play of boys and girls.

Feminism

Prior to the late nineteenth century, there were pockets of interest in feminism, which has at its core a belief in equality of the sexes, despite the fact that it originally appeared to focus solely on women. At the heart of current interest in gender and sexuality lies the feminist movement. Feminism can be viewed in many ways. It can be seen as a philosophy, a social movement, a political stance or a way of thinking. Women such as Hildegarde of Bingen, Mary Wollstonecraft and Jane Austen are seen as the forerunners of the modern women's movement, because they defied convention and followed their own paths. According to Rampton (2008), the first wave of modern feminism came out of the second industrial or technical revolution of the country and the liberalizing of the social politics of the early twentieth century. The idea behind this was to open up opportunities for women and the suffragettes were particularly important to this as organizations of female activists who fought hard to gain votes for women. The Representation of the People Act 1928 was eventually passed, giving all women over twenty-one the same voting rights as men. The cult of domesticity was challenged and women's new participation in politics led to discussions about differences between men and women – some claiming women to be morally superior!

Feminism enjoyed a revival in the 1960s. This unfolded in the context of the anti-war and civil rights movements and a growing awareness of there being a variety of underprivileged, under-represented minority groups around the world, of which women were one. Women sought sisterhood with other women around the world and aligned their struggle for equality with class and race struggles. Feminism became increasingly radical and theoretical. Sexuality and reproductive rights became important issues.

Reflective question

What changes related to reproductive rights have occurred in your lifetime?

Women's groups began to associate control of women with the broader notions of patriarchy, capitalism, heterosexuality as normal and a woman's role as 'wife and mother'. There were efforts made on a number of fronts to rid society of sexism, from children's cartoons, books and clothes across the layers of our culture, through to our laws and government. Holland (2003/08: 9) says that during this time: 'Perceived sexist patterns in children's play clearly presented themselves as an area in which women could take some control.' In the mid-1980s, in-service training for people who worked in the early years' sector, focused on anti-sexist practices. The 'Wendy house' was considered a sexist description for an area in which both boys and girls could play and 'home corner' was substituted instead. There was a campaign of zero tolerance to war, weapon and superhero play as it was considered to be linked to adult male violence, domestic abuse and rape. Feminists and women liberationists from many campaigning groups all believed that nurture had a larger part to play than nature and that if you took the guns away from boys and substituted them with dolls, boys could be socialized away from models of violence at an early age. (As you will see from Chapter 6 this is no longer considered the case, although now there is a concern about clothes and song lyrics as being corrupting.) Many women began to see themselves as a collective of more caring, collaborative, inclusive, peaceful, nurturing, democratic people than men, with a more holistic way of solving problems and with a greater connection to the earth.

Since the 1970s, some men have also become aware that they, too, are the object of sexism. Not all men want to be the breadwinners, the strong, powerful, unemotional, driven, logical ones in relation to heterosexual coupledom, responsible for earning money and providing protection for their woman or family. They recognize that they have many of the traits that are considered to be feminine and/or they enjoy some or many of the aspects of life normally carried out by women, such as child rearing, homemaking and the like. At the very least, some men, but by no means all, started to recognize the need for sharing of all aspects of life in an equal and fair way. However difficult men have found, or might still find some aspects of their gendered life, as yet they have not suffered the long years of oppression that women have and women, generally, are still far more disadvantaged by inequality than men.

Some feminist ideologies were, and still are, considered dangerous and/ or misguided by both men and women. The term 'political correctness' continues to be used as a derogatory term for some of the attempts, legal and non-legal, to change inappropriate language and practices associated with mainly racism and sexism, which some people believe are a step too far.

Reflective question

Can you think of any examples of this and what are your views?

Rampton (2008) tells us a third phase of feminism began from the mid-1990s, informed by post-modern thinking and challenging many of the constructs of the second wave, including notions of universal womanhood, body image, gender, sexuality and heteronormativity. Today, many young feminists wear lipstick, high heels and sexy clothing, items previously associated with male oppression. These women view themselves as individuals and girls sometimes see themselves as having 'girl power' and define their own feminine beauty for themselves as subjects, rather than objects of men's desire. Currently, there is much more ambiguity relating to gender and sex and third-wave feminism embraces this. Many second-wave feminists view some of this as retrograde steps and feel there has been no progress relating to such things as the pay gap, too few women in positions of real power and so on; they are worried about a slide back to old ways. There is also a concern that society is in a downward spiral, with children becoming increasingly sexualized and genderized despite modern women feminists believing themselves to be strong and empowered and not victims. Feminist philosophy and the rest of society's thinking do not always match up. Rampton (2008) suggested that the feminist movement has always been confused and has had too many different branches – and this still seems true today.

However, what we do know is that despite the fact there are many people who either do not even consider feminist rhetoric or who think that feminism is dangerous, silly or wrong, feminism has done much to create greater equality and to change the way that we think about men, women and society. This includes an awareness of issues that may or may not contribute to inequality, such as the way that boys and girls play and aspects of children's culture. There is, however, still much to be done!

Masculinity and femininity

Lippa (2005) gives us a brief history of varying tests that have been devised and developed across the modern period (1920s to 2000s), to look at masculinity and femininity as perceived by different psychologists. These traits became of interest alongside the rise in feminism and equality between the sexes. He states (2005: 49) that Teman and Miles proposed a 'bipolar' approach to masculinity and femininity in the 1920s and invented a test that was used up until the 1970s, which apparently determined whether you were masculine or feminine. Lippa (2005: 55) further tells us that in 1973, Constantinople suggested that masculinity and femininity were 'amongst the muddiest concepts in the psychologists vocabulary'. Bem (1983) believed many people were androgynous and viewed these people as able to utilize masculine and feminine aspects of themselves: she devised an inventory of masculine and feminine traits that could test people across a sliding scale of instrumental and expressive traits.

Lippa (2005: 63–5) asserts that in the 1990s Wiggins came up with five dimensions to human personality; namely extraversion, agreeableness, conscientiousness, neuroticism and openness to experience. He found that masculinity had strong overlaps with extraversion and neuroticism and femininity with agreeableness and, to a lesser degree, conscientiousness. He, therefore, suggested that masculinity and femininity did not measure separate personality traits, but rather were aspects of other personality characteristics. At this time, Bem also came up with 'Gender Schema Theory', which changed gender from being seen as individual traits, but instead showed how society tended to measure gender in a bipolar way as either more masculine or feminine depending upon such things as clothes, body movements, hobbies, employment, etc. which she termed 'cultural fictions'.

Reflective question

Do you see any children using clothes, body movements, hobbies or role-play etc. as a mark of being a male or female?

Psychologists now see masculine and feminine as much more 'fuzzy' concepts, but Lippa (2005: 67) thinks that just because they are multi-faceted, it does not mean that they are meaningless and do not exist, rather that they are complex. He has come up with his own 'Gender Diagnosticity' theory. This approach works out the probability that a person is male or female, based on pieces of information that distinguish men and women in a particular group, in a particular culture and during a particular period. In this way the test acknowledges that masculinity and femininity are to some extent historically and culturally relative, but are, nevertheless, still something to be considered in relation to individuals.

Reflective question

Would you consider that there are masculine and feminine traits and if so, what do you think they are?

FIGURE 2.1 *Witch and wizard, equal in play*
Permission granted by Peach and Statham

Is there equality in boys and girls play?

How is all this interest in equality of the sexes reflected in children's play? In play differences and play styles? Despite the fact many changes do happen, and there have been societal changes, if we look back at some historical accounts relating to boys and girls in Britain, we can see that in some ways very little has changed, despite society's new interest in gender equality. As we can see from Chapter 1, play is very important in the lives of children – and differences in the play of boys and girls are not just noted in British society, but across the world. According to Cunningham (2006: 33), in medieval times, Bartholomew of England wrote of small boys that they were:

> without thought or care, loving only to play, fearing no danger [...] always hungry and disposed to illness as a result of greed, resisting their mothers' efforts to wash and comb them, and no sooner clean than dirty again.

Little girls he thought were 'more careful, more modest and timid and more easily disciplined'.

Reflective questions

What rights or opportunities are missing from either or both of the sexes here? Do these views still persist?

Certainly, despite strides that have been made towards equality, we have heard views of this kind expressed in recent times. Cunningham (2006: 87) further tells us that 'in 1642 a Sir Justinian Isham wrote a code of conduct for his four daughters exhorting them to 'have regard for the behaviour that the sacred scriptures direct them to as proper for their sex: holiness, meekness, discretion, chastity, modesty, frugality, obedience, sobriety, affability, charity and silence'. There seem to be some, in our society, who still expect this of their daughters, yet not of their sons. With the expansion of public schools in the mid-nineteenth century and an emphasis on games-playing, Cunningham (2006: 144) also tells us that the manly boy was expected to be physically tough and repress his emotions. Apparently this idea needed to be instilled at an early age, so many middle-class boys were sent away to school while they were very young.

Have you ever heard a parent saying to their little boy 'be a brave boy, don't cry!' or something similar?

Although some aspects of life relating to the roles that men and women fulfil in society has changed, has the way that boys and girls are brought up, how they are expected to behave and how they play also changed in relation to this?

Some people – Shibley-Hyde (2005), Leaper and Smith (2004) – consider there are more similarities between males and females than there are differences. However, if we consider a range of accounts of children's play, we can see that there are many who note differences in the way that girls and boys play and have played across recent historical times. Cranwell (1999) recounts, in his article about street play and games between 1880 and 1920, that Anna Davin (1995), in her book, *Growing up Poor*, argues that there were gender differences between girls' and boys' play. This was because girls were expected to take a bigger part in household chores and had less time for leisure. Girls, then, were also expected to conform to female gender stereotypes – while working-class girls did tidying, cleaning and looked after siblings and middle-class girls did embroidery, water colours and played the piano, all of them were expected to be subservient to men. In their collected works on children's play, Opie and Opie (1977) sometimes talk of 'children's' games and rhymes, but often attribute them to either 'girls' or 'boys'. They say (1977: 346):

> Boys are definitely realists: The characteristic they most want in a friend is that he should like playing the same games that they do. 'My best friend is John Corbett [...] we both draw spaceships. When we are playing rocket ships he never starts laughing when we get to an awkward bit'.

The Opies also report that 'Little girls are highly conscious of their friends' appearance: "Dulcie has got lovely hair, that's partly why I like her."' Abrams (1997: 106/7) asserts that:

> whilst boys tend to play games that develop motor skills, provide organizational skills and involve competition with others, girls tend to play games that teach sensitivity, consideration and empathy. (By the age of three, she says), these differences are clearly noticeable with boys more likely to play active aggressive games with more hitting and pushing, while girls are more likely to be found having pretend tea parties, brushing each other's hair, playing with dolls and dressing up.

Katch (2001: 59) notices that both girls and boys can be mean to their friends or leave people out, but notes that the 'girls" exclusion is quieter than that of the boys' noisy quarrels.' Maccoby (2003: 72), in her chapter summary on cross-sex encounters, states 'Girls – especially in early childhood – tend to be wary of interacting with boys. Many find boys' play styles too rough.' Most of these views seem to concur with the historical perceptions found in Cunningham's *History of Childhood*. Maccoby (2003: 179), however, has 'no doubt that children make self-regulating efforts to adapt themselves to child culture', as she notes that gender segregation in childhood is not a matter of children imitating what they see adults doing. She does think however, that what children play in their segregated groups is heavily determined by the 'gendered scripts their culture provides'.

Reflective question

D o you agree with Maccoby that different cultures at different times have different gendered scripts that impact on children's play?

We believe that in current Western society there are fewer and different social scripts that are sex distinctive than there used to be, or that are found, in more traditional societies.

Reflective questions

W hat do you think? Which sex distinctive social scripts have you seen being played by children?

Eliot (2010: 113) tells us that it seems that few children engage predominantly in cross-gender play, but a certain amount of experimentation with opposite gender behaviour is normal at different ages. In relation to children's own thoughts, Bead (1994: 106) thinks that age plays a critical part in exaggerated gender stereotyping. She suggests, for instance, that: '4yr olds think it is fine for a boy to wear a dress but 5 and 6yr olds are critical, yet 9 & 10 yr olds are accepting' [*sic*].

What examples have you experienced of children playing across the genders?

What causes girls and boys to play differently, or to be perceived as playing differently by some people, is the subject matter of other chapters. However, we shall consider whether this difference in playing, if there truly is such, has any particular significance for girls and boys during and after they play.

In Chapter 1, we have talked about the importance of play itself. But play might be either gendered or genderized and whether this is significant depends upon one's point of view. Some second-wave feminists, for example, consider children's gendered or genderized play will have a negative influence on their lives and they, therefore, try to influence or prevent it from happening. Some scientists, including Becker et al. (2008: 275), consider that:

these differences (in boys and girls gendered or genderized play) emerge early in life, and are among the largest non-reproductive physical or psychological differences (between male and female children) [...] the differences have considerable significance for mental health, social relationships and cognition across the life span.

Similarly, Berenbaum et al. (2008: 286) conclude that:

Sex differences in childhood play are important for many reasons [...] they are large, they lead to sex differences in other characteristics (including cognition and adjustment), they reflect the joint effects of biological predispositions, the social world and children's constructions of that world. These differences also have indirect long-term consequences. Children's environments are changed as a result of their play and this in turn affects later opportunities. This means the lives of girls and boys are differently channelled, constrained, or expanded as a result of early differences.

This view – that play, of any sort, affects how children develop and eventually turn out – could be particularly scary if you are aware that: the children in your care are playing in stereotypically gendered or genderized ways; that there is a power differential between adult males and females in our society; or if you are concerned that gendered play is part of the problem relating to the sexualization of childhood or feel that both males and females are suffering from a lack of equal rights. The notion that what

Berenbaum calls 'children's environments' (we interpret this to mean the imaginary worlds they inhabit, which, in turn, allow them to see their real world differently) are changed as a result of their stereotypically gendered play is also worrying if you believe that this change has implications for their future. Should we be paying attention to this? Or do we believe that play is only about the here and now? Feminists and people who believe that all gendered behaviour is socialized into children certainly argue that stereotypically male or female play behaviour is harmful. However, others think not; they believe that differences are hard wired and gendered play is just a manifestation of this. We will discuss this further in Chapters 3 and 4.

There are some who wonder if there are benefits to children developing gender-stereotyped roles? Most people who work with children know that play is very important, but does anyone think that stereotypically gendered play is important? Eliot (2010: 113) wonders, '[i]f each sex sticks to its own gender-appropriate play (what exactly this is, is a matter for discussion), children wind up strengthening those same brain areas that were already biased to work better from birth'. Gender becomes an organizing principle for children, helping them understand and interpret the behaviours of those around them.

Eliot thinks that there may be a cost to encouraging girls to play more with stereotypical boys' toys, because they will play some of the time with boys' toys anyway, but time use, in childhood play, is limited to certain periods during that childhood and there may be benefits to playing with girls' toys that we are not aware of. The same may be true when encouraging boys to play with stereotypical girls' toys. There are particular skills associated with different types of play and some are specifically associated with gender. Does providing boys with construction and transport toys give them an advantage over girls? Do these toys represent some kind of power? Does providing girls with dolls and pushchairs give them an advantage over boys? Do these toys imbue the players with some kind of power? Do they nurture some kind of ability in the players to care for people? Do gender roles serve an important social and psychological function for individuals, as well as society, or are they, as some people (mainly women) think, a way of keeping a power differential in favour of men? There are certainly those who would say so. It is rare that you hear views expressed that suggest that pink, pretty or domestic-type toys imbue children with power. In an extract from *Cinderella Ate my Daughter* Orenstein (*Observer* 2011), wonders whether she should see this mania for pink princesses as being some kind of progress, where girls can celebrate their power, strength and independence through the colour pink.

Reflective questions

What do you think? Is gender-stereotypical play okay or not okay and why?

Sexualization of childhood

What of the notion of sexualization of childhood in Britain and other countries? Sexuality and gender are intertwined. Are modern feminists, with their overtly sexual images, inadvertently colluding with what Bailey (2011: 14) refers to as 'the wallpaper of children's lives', which he suggests is filled with sexual images? Papadopoulos (2010: 6) states that '[s]exualization is the imposition of adult sexuality on to children and young people before they are capable of dealing with it, mentally, emotionally or physically'. When Papadopoulos talks of 'adult sexuality', is she talking about 'sexual orientation' – same-sex or opposite-sex sexual attraction, desire and sexual behaviour? Or is she talking about sexual identity? How we view ourselves or how our public sexual identity is expressed and how others look at it? Papadopoulos suggests that while the democratization of sex and sexuality may appear to break down the binary oppositions of, for example, heterosexuality and homosexuality, the commercialization of sexuality has involved the use of feminist terminology – empowerment, girl power, etc. – and serves to reinforce male domination by ensuring that 'female sexual expression gains validity under the surveillance of men'. Bailey (2011) reports on the very strong concerns that parents express about their children's early sexualization. Parents are concerned that their children are growing up too quickly; taking part in a sexualized life before they are ready and being bombarded by consumerism of a genderized nature.

Reflective questions

Do you think that this is the case? Do you agree with the sentiment?

Papadopoulos suggests that such things as gender, class and age are being used to exaggerate constructions of femininity and masculinity; she sees children as being adultified, while adult women are being infantilized and boys are being hyper-masculinized. She does not say that children are being homosexualized!

Interestingly, neither Papadopoulos's (2010) nor Bailey's (2011) reviews about the sexualization of childhood, mention anything about the 'heteronormativity' of our culture and the difficulties that some young people may have in relation to this. Bem (1998: 159) has suggested that there is a 'cultural belief that men are naturally masculine, women are naturally feminine, and everyone is naturally heterosexual'. There is, seemingly, greater acceptance of a range of sexualities in our modern society that are evidenced by such things as the development of anti-sexist laws and more open LGBT (Lesbian, Gay, Bi and Transgender) support and interest organizations and venues. There has been an upsurge in celebrities divulging a range of their sexualities and the media has sensationalized aspects of this. Latterly, cast into law, there is the opportunity for authorized same-sex partnerships and very recently this has developed into the opportunity for gay people to marry, thus allowing them to join mainstream culture. However, concerns about children's sexual orientation and public expressions of sexual identity did not feature in Bailey's Review, commissioned by the coalition government. Is this because members of society, including the children themselves, accept and embrace the idea that we all develop along a spectrum of gender and sexuality which has at one extreme, male/female/ heterosexual and at the other gender/queer/gay/lesbian/transgender/homosexual/bisexual? We would like to think so, but we are not sure that this is the case.

Despite the fact that according to Hines (2004: 124) there is 'no evidence that even dramatically cross-gendered activities in childhood cause adult homosexuality', it would seem that many parents, particularly fathers relating to their sons, do fear children playing in opposing gender ways. Could this be because they fear their child may be socialized to become gay? Or because they fear it as a sign of gayness? Hines (2004: 122–4) gives examples of numerous studies that suggest that homosexual men and women engaged more in extreme cross-sex play and cross-dressing than heterosexual men and women. However, homosexuality is not a 'choice' that a child makes. In whichever way a child plays, they will express their sexuality according to their own desires. According to Picavet and Reinders (2006), homosexual men and women usually feel that their sexual orientation is inevitable. Green (1987) found that when they interviewed their child subjects later in life, as young adults, his researchers found that 75 per cent of the effeminate boys, who had engaged in what they then termed as 'gender inappropriate play', had become gay in adulthood, despite pressure from peers and family to adhere to gender norms, thereby suggesting that this was not learned behaviour.

Schuhrke (2000: 1537) tells us that 'although each child comes to form his or her sexuality in a unique way, there are patterns of sexuality formation common for both boys and girls'. He explains that quite young children become aware of how bodies look and work and through exploring their own body become aware of it as part of themselves and their identity. However, Walkerdine (1989) in Harrison and Hood-Williams (2002: 151) writes that the child only 'believes itself [sic] to have chosen that which is really being imposed upon it externally'. This would suggest that although the child believes themself to be the originator of their own actions, in actuality gendered and sexualized play has been imposed on them by society and the culture in which they lives.

Do you believe that this is the case?

Does it matter?

In *Delusions of Gender* (2011: 123), primatologist Frances Burton is cited as proposing 'that the effect of foetal hormones in primates is to predispose them to be receptive to whatever behaviours happen to go with their own sex in the particular society into which they are born'. Hines thinks this would 'liberate' the primates from 'hard-wired' masculinity or femininity, so that the behaviour would be adaptive to changing circumstances in the society. If our society is becoming generally more genderized and sexualized, should we be concerned that children reflect this through their play? There are some who are very concerned, but others who either ignore or embrace these aspects of modern culture.

Reflective question

Do you think it matters?

We will go on in further chapters to discuss why we think it might.

Suggested reading

Eliot, Lise (2010), *Pink Brain Blue Brain*, One World Publications.
Fine, Cordelia (2011), *Delusions of Gender*, London: Icon Books.
Picavet, C. and J. Reinders (2004), *Sexual Orientation and Young People*, Utrecht, The Netherlands: Colophon–Youth Incentives/Rutgers Nisso Groep.

CHAPTER THREE

Boys and girls playing: Same or different?

Introduction

In this chapter, we will look briefly at what scientists say about gender similarities and differences in children's play and go on to compare these with real life examples of playing. We have both conducted many observations of children playing and gathered anecdotes and observations from a range of children's workers and parents. We will share and reflect on a few of these in the light of the scientists' conclusions and will examine their evidence in greater depth in Chapter 4.

We need to lay some sort of foundation for why it is that so many people believe so strongly that there either are or are not differences between the behaviour of boys and girls and, particularly, in their play behaviour. Studies across the world and over time have consistently noted gender differences in the ways in which children play and parents anecdotally continue to agree: but is this really true and what part does nature or nurture have in this? Ackerley (2003: 11) asserts: 'If observers concentrate their observations on distinct gender groupings, then results will be different to observations with a focus on interaction between the two groups.' There are also researchers who believe that if you are looking for difference in the behaviour of boys and girls, you will find it, but that actually, there are more similarities than differences in the ways in which boys and girls play.

Reflective questions

Do some people think there are differences between the way that boys and girls play because that is what they want to think or is it because that is what they have seen? Is it possible to separate those two things?

Maccoby (2003: 32) succinctly states: 'Playful behaviour is not something directly taught by the older generation to the younger. Nor is it something young creatures learn by watching the behaviour of their parents'. Play is the domain of children and Maccoby suggests that play is 'an emergent activity' and a 'major enterprise' of childhood. Thus, while they play, children's ideas about gender emerge as part of that enterprise.

Whatever we may wish to think about gender difference, there is consistent 'evidence' from research undertaken from different fields, such as developmental, educational and child psychology, neuroscience, early years and education that boys and girls do play differently and some differences emerge and change over time (Maccoby (2003), Eliot (2010), Hines (2004), Martin (2011), Holland (2003/08), Smith (2010), Becker et al. (2008), Sax (2005), Blatchford et al. (2003), Pellegrini et al. (2004) – and even from people who might prefer to think otherwise, see Karsten (2003), Jordan-Young (2011) Davies (1997). Indeed, some believe play behaviours to be the biggest gender difference of all. It is believed that boys and girls choose to play at and with different things in different ways and that after the age of about three or four, they tend to choose more play partners from their own sex than the other. Many of you may immediately disagree and, indeed, from the discipline of behavioural science, Aydt and Corsaro (2003: 1309) suggest that most studies have only looked at middle-class white children and that their results cannot, therefore, be generalized to all children. Other researchers from a range of fields such as neuroscience, anthropology, developmental neuropsychology and psychology, however, (for example, Eliot [2010], Whiting and Edwards [1988], Berenbaum et al. [2008] and Smith [2010]) see play differences as being universal. It is neither a comfortable thought for some, nor their reality, that boys and girls play differently and depending upon your perspective, neither is it fixed. What potentially causes these assumed differences is the subject of great debate as you will see in Chapter 4, but *statistically*, in the research that we have consulted, there is no doubt that there are differences in the play behaviour of boys and girls. For those of you who are having trouble with this, keep in mind that statistics may change depending upon circumstances! For instance in Meire's (n.d.: 6) qualitative research on children's play, he tells us that: 'A surprisingly large amount of gender-related play research is conducted in school playgrounds' – Thomson (2005); Pellegrini et al. (2004); Goodwin (2001); Evaldsson (2003); Blatchford et al. (2003); Riley and Jones (2005); Ackerley (2003) (and we add Thorne [1993/2009]). This should be noticed, since school playgrounds are (in his view) very specifically gendered settings: gender segregation appears to be much sharper there than in other contexts such as street play in children's neighbourhoods.

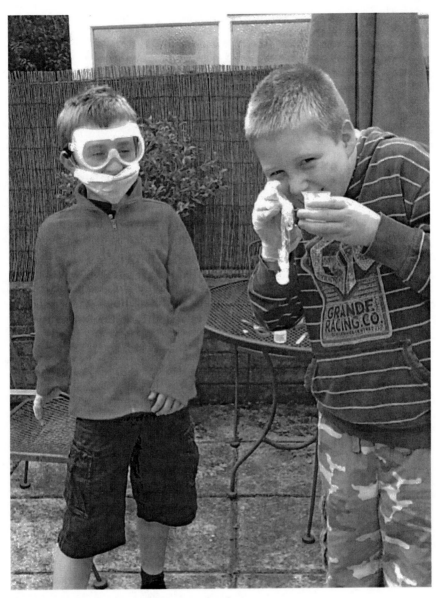

FIGURE 3.1 *What are little boys made of?*
Permission granted by Peach and Marcer

Reflective questions

Do you think that school playgrounds are gendered settings and if so, why? Have you been able to compare the play behaviour of children in school playgrounds to that of children playing in other settings, such as adventure playgrounds, nurseries, at home, in the neighbourhood, at a playscheme, in a crèche, and so on?

Fine (2010: 128) says that 'children are attracted to things and behaviours associated with their sex' and (2011: 211) she states that developmental psychologists Martin and Ruble, suggest that children become 'gender detectives', trying to find clues as to the implications of belonging to the 'male or female tribes'. If children themselves are interested in things that are particularly associated with their own sex, it would seem likely that they would not only initiate different forms of play depending upon how they perceive male and female and where they fit in, but also perpetuate it.

We will begin by looking at what many of the scientists state are differences between the play behaviours of boys and girls. In brief these are:

1 **Play styles**

Boys:

● play outdoors

● in large groups

● rush about

Girls:

● more often indoors

● usually in smaller groups or pairs

● participate more in talking and discussion

2 **Physical play**

Boys:

● are more physical

● take up more space when they play

● like rough-and-tumble play

● are more physically aggressive between themselves

● show more attempts at dominance

● are generally more competitive

Girls:

- use smaller spaces
- take up less space
- are more likely to take turns
- dominate through leadership skills rather than by physical domination

3   Themes for pretend play

Boys:

- like heroic and war-like themes
- imitate or dress up in superhero and villain outfits
- use things as weapons for killing or rescuing

Girls:

- take on much more familial and domestic roles
- like to dress up to be glamorous
- take on other female roles such as princesses and fairies, e.g. girly outfits, dresses, make-up and accessories

4   Activities and interests

Boys:

- like diggers and trucks and things that move
- play organized sports (participation and watching)
- like to construct and deconstruct things
- are interested in adventure stories

Girls:

- are interested in many of the same things as boys
- also like arts and crafts; clothes, romance and family orientated stories

5   Groups

Boys:

- are more likely to try to dominate their group
- get on with their own thing
- tease boys who do 'girly' things

● don't try to join girls' groups

Girls:

● are generally more collaborative and agreement is reached more easily

● are more likely to include boys if they want to be included

● do play stereotypical boy activities

● join boys' groups more readily

6 **Friendships**

Boys:

● have more paired friendships

● are often involved in big groups based on shared activities

Girls:

● have mainly reciprocal intimate friendships in pairs

● often have 'best friends'

● have small groups of friends

However let's be clear here – this does not mean that all boys and/or all girls do all these things! But, according to the research to date, the majority do, even if their parents feel they have been 'gender-neutral' in their toy purchases and child-rearing.

Reflective questions

How do you react to this? Will you find the same results from your own and others observations and viewpoints?

Below we will share a few of the observations we have gathered, in order to compare our experience with that of the scientists who have studied gender in some detail.

Observations and anecdotal examples

1. Play styles

Example 1.1

At an adventure playground with both indoor and outdoor facilities during a hot day, inside – seven girls were involved with drawing and printing with sponges in the arts and crafts area, while five boys were playing pool and another boy was playing table tennis with a male playworker. This changed to two girls playing table tennis and three different boys playing pool. Outside, two boys instigated a water fight by throwing a bowl of water at a playworker and soon a large group of boys and playworkers, including one female playworker were engaged in a water fight. Only one small girl (the daughter of the female playworker) fully joined in – a few older girls lurked excitedly on the edges, but did not get wet. Six boys played football in the multi-use area. Seven young children (aged about three to five), four boys and three girls played on the swinging roundabout. They played together, stopping carefully when a very little girl wanted to get off. Three older boys came in and started ranging around, one playing a drum and one wheeling about on a wheelie board. They asked to use the bikes, but these were not available that day.

Example 1.2

At an after-school club with indoor and outdoor facilities, children arrived in different groups, from different parts of two schools. Four children came in first, three girls and a boy. One girl went to the construction table and made an object that she began shooting with. She marched about the room, saying, 'I've got a weapon'. She offered it to me, but I declined it and suggested she offered it to another little girl instead, who was sitting quietly drawing. 'It's a weapon. She doesn't like these,' she said to me. 'I'm the boss.' However, she did end up giving it to the girl, repeating the words, 'It's a weapon. I'm the boss.' She gave me another, saying, 'This is your weapon. Keep it there and use it or you can draw round it. L's [a woman] the boss and she'll be really angry.' (I was not sure whether the girl meant because she had made a weapon, but L clearly had no problem with it.)

Two more groups of children came in: one group had four girls and the other had thirteen boys and one girl. The noise levels shot up when the boys came in and started singing and shouting. A lot of the children raced outside. After some banter and shouting between two different groups of boys, one located inside the playground at the after-school club and the other standing outside on a path, ten boys started playing football in the playground. All the girls, who had left the building, went back inside. Two boys played inside with dinosaurs that roared at each other; one boy was making a Lego spaceship and another boy played on the computer. A boy and a girl played at dressing up, the boy as Dracula and the girl wearing a fireman's hat. Other girls were drawing or chatting together. Back outside the now eight boys played football, taking up the larger part of the playground, and, on the periphery of their game, four girls built a wooden train track and two boys and one girl played with other dinosaurs. Two girls, one of whom was carrying the 'weapon', came out carrying two tents. The weapon was given to me to look after and she then started playing with the girls with the train track. Two girls put sheets over the erected tents and went inside one. The boys and girl with the dinosaurs took them inside the other tent. Six boys were still playing football using most of the playground. A father came to pick up his daughter, one of the girls in charge of constructing the train track. He asked her 'Why aren't you playing football?'. She replied 'Because I've been playing it all day at school.'

We are sure that you have your own examples of what you consider to be children playing in gendered and/or non-gendered play styles. To attempt to get to the bottom of this, it is important to recognize our own attitudes and beliefs and try to interpret everything that we see and hear with fresh eyes and ears. At first glance, members of the group in Example 1.1 could be interpreted as exhibiting mainly stereotypically gendered play behaviour – the boys were rushing about and playing with water and football outside, the girls were at the craft table inside and both girls and boys were primarily playing in segregated groups. In Example 1.2, however, there are examples of cross-gender and non-gendered play behaviour. A girl was playing with weapons; several girls were playing with a train track, both usually considered 'boys toys' and there were also girls and boys playing together with dinosaurs (which boys tend to do more) and dressing up (which girls tend to do more).

If we look at these examples again, we could interpret aspects of the first observation differently. There were a group of boys and girls playing together outside on the roundabout and the older girls may have been 'lurking around' the periphery of the water fight because:

- they were working out tactics;

- the boys were dominating which made it difficult for the girls to get in even if they wanted to; or

- there were three male playworkers and only one female playworker playing so the workers were role modelling 'boys play', which might mean that the girls were less likely to join in.

We could also interpret aspects of the second observation differently. The girl playing with 'the weapon' was very vocal about it, rather than just making it and playing with it: perhaps she was told that weapons were inappropriate to play with and she was reacting to that. She might have done the same thing with a Barbie doll if she were told that was inappropriate to play with – so, this might not be an example of gendered play, but rather 'power' play. Although a boy and girl were dressing up together, the girl was choosing a 'male' outfit and the group consisted of two boys and a girl playing with dinosaurs, creatures more readily associated with 'boys" games. As will be seen later in the chapter, it is common for some girls to crossover into boys' games, but far less common for boys to crossover into girls' games. There was a large group of boys playing football and taking up most of the space outside and this is very stereotypically boys' play behaviour.

There could be other interpretations of all of the above stories – it depends on how open our views are to interpreting what should be classed as data. Of course, this presupposes that what has been recorded is actually an accurate record of what went on – perhaps the observation was biased in the first place! And in reality all we see is the physical manifestations of playing on one isolated occasion – how can we possibly know what children – of either sex – are thinking and feeling when they play and why that might be?

2. Physical play

Example 2.1

An adventure playground was given some long foam rolls (the kind used as floats in swimming pools). Several lads, aged between about nine- to twelve-years old, played a game with them over several days. Each boy took turns to be the victim and the others would chase him all over the playground, eventually catching him and then battering him with the rolls. The victim would curl up to try to fend off the worst of the attack, but would take it without complaining (although despite being foam, it clearly hurt). The battering then stopped and, after a few minutes rest, another victim volunteered and the chase and consequent assault began again. The playworkers monitored this, occasionally asking if the victim was okay, but all the boys seemed immersed in the game and wanted it to continue – it seemed rather like a rite of passage. Eventually, after several days, the game intensified, seeming to take over the playground and becoming more brutal; other children became frightened and some parents expressed concern. One of the victims received a nasty ear injury, so the playworkers stopped the game altogether.

Example 2.2

A group of girls, aged between nine and ten, found a pile of long, white elastic in the Scrapstore Playpod in their school playground. The girls made a 'boxing ring' by stretching lengths of this elastic around two trees and two fence posts. They then, with much laughter, proceeded to fight, holding wrestling matches and sword fights, using long cardboard tubes. They spent as much time organizing and re-planning these mock battles as they did fighting and regularly burst into giggles throughout.

Both of these interesting examples comprise elements of aggression and both are very physical (characteristics that are reputedly male), yet both require a high degree of co-operation (a characteristic reputedly female). The boys' game uses more space during the chasing and appears to be quite wild, while the girls' game is confined to a specific created space, giving it the appearance of greater control. The girls also verbally plan and discuss what to do and how to be throughout, as though they are staging a drama and trying out wrestling roles. In their play, the boys demonstrate group dominance over one boy at a time, but each of them take a turn at playing victim which might suggest they are 'practicing' both endurance and oppression. Are we seeing the greater effects of testosterone at work here? Or are these boys (who are growing up in a very tough neighbourhood) finding ways through their play to survive – they may be not staging a drama, but perhaps living one. For us, neither of these examples show just stereotypical gendered behaviour, but illustrate children's active agency in their interactions.

3. Themes for pretend play

Example 3.1

In a school playground, with access to a range of loose parts, a dozen boys formed two armies, created strategies and 'attacked' each other with cardboard rolls, rushing and shouting at each other across the playground with a mixture of laughter and seriousness. The armies took prisoners and then negotiated satisfactory release terms before the next 'raid'.

Example 3.2

On an adventure playground, several girls found piles of donated white net curtains and proceeded to dress up. They took turns to be brides and 'marry' each other, repeating their own made-up vows and making a hilarious show of kissing their forearms, rather than each other. They also 'divorced' each other, with one of them acting as a court judge so that they could then 'remarry'.

Example 3.3

Jacky has a particular play relationship with one of her grandsons, whose family she visits every two or three months. They have an elaborate game that they started when he was four and which continues on during his eighth year. The game has developed across the years and ranges across a whole variety of play types. It incorporates domestic, familial, superhero, villainous, war, television and therapeutic themes that are, at times, aggressive and at times nurturing. The game uses an increasing number of play resources over the years including soft toys, Lego, small world figures and their associated equipment, household items (used both as themselves and symbolically), toy kitchen equipment and paper and pens and is always played in her grandson's bedroom. If unavoidable, the game can incorporate Jacky's younger grandson, too, but this often causes a tussle for dominance between the two boys. The game started originally with the older grandson being Mr Incredible, Jacky playing his wife and three soft toys embodying their children. The first incarnation of the game included Mr Incredible carrying out superhero feats, as well as running a pizza parlour for birthday parties, but now includes a variety of role play, such as James Bond (who sometimes disguises himself) and some children cook him disgusting meals and then get punished severely; accidents that require hospitalization, police and the fire service; boats surrounded by water and sharks; discos, and on. This wide-ranging game is only played when Jacky is with her grandsons and the game has a wonderful nonsensical sentence, a password that is growing and which is used alternatively as a form of secret code, admonition and a way of producing laughter.

The game between Jacky and her grandson both contains themes that could be considered male – superheroes, villains and rescuing – and also themes that could be considered female – family, cooking, parties – all of which, in turn, are dictated by a boy. The only stereotypical aspect of the game is that the grandson is always the man, while Jacky's role varies; she is sometimes told to be a woman, sometimes a man. She notes that the tussle for dominance between her older grandson and his brother when the latter plays is probably more associated with sibling rivalry than with anything to do with gender. Perhaps when we use words to describe whether things seem masculine (of the male variety) or feminine (of the female variety), in actuality, children's play behaviour ranges across a continuum of both and, therefore, should be thought of as neither.

Examples 3.1 and 3.2 are very stereotypical of the pretend play themes imagined by boys and girls, with the boys playing at war and the girls playing at weddings. But within these simple themes the children's narratives do reveal a more complex and changing story, with children exploring the theme rather than necessarily being fashioned by it.

4. Activities and interests

Example 4.1

A mother of two young boys, aged two and five, told us: 'My two are definitely drawn to boys' dressing up clothes and boys' toys and now do a mock scream at anything pink and cry, "Arggggggh ... *Barbie*!" – as if they are under attack! Apparently, neither of them has been tempted to wear the girl/girlish dressing up clothes at their nursery, which has a rail with a complete range of outfits and at which the staff just let them pick whatever they wish. We get shot at, lazered and tazered during role play and they fall over in mock death and shout about killing others and/or each other. A batman figure is never cuddled or held affectionately, he's tossed across the room or crashed into a fake building or thrown off an imaginary bridge in an explosion.'

Example 4.2

A three-year-old boy, when asked what he would like to do for his fourth birthday party, decided that he would like to go to an arts and crafts place, where children can make and paint their own artefacts. He chose three boys and three girls as the friends that he would like to invite.

Example 4.3

Another mother of four talked to us about her five-year-old daughter, who has three older brothers. 'I think she must have been swapped with another family's daughter at birth, because she's just so girly and it doesn't make sense. I'm not like that – I'm not into fashion or make-up or anything and her brothers are typical boys, but since she was little (and she never went to nursery and so hardly ever played with other girls), she has always been fascinated by dresses and hair and dolls – where does all that come from?!'

Examples 4.1 and 4.3 show us two little boys and a girl who fit every gender stereotype going, yet the boy in Example 4.2 chose an activity which was supposedly much more typical of girls than of boys. All four of these children are still young, of course, and their attitudes towards gender-related activity may, of course, change over time: we are only seeing a snapshot of their self-expression in the present moment.

Fine (2010: 205) tells us of a study in which gender differences in play were recorded in one-year-old boys and girls. Although the boys spent more time with boyish toys, 'the sexes spent a similar amount of time with girlish toys and were equally likely to choose a ball, a doll or a car as a gift from the experimenter'. Fine also tells us (2010: 230) that at seventeen months, boy and girl toddlers were equally interested in dolls, tea sets, brush-and-comb sets and blocks, but by twenty-one months, girls had increased their doll play and boys had decreased it. These are examples of non-stereotypical gendered play gradually being supplanted by gender stereotypical play. Fine also gives examples of how toys and games can be made attractive to either sex merely by suggesting that they are, thereby demonstrating that the play of boys and girls might be more similar if they did not live within a gendered world.

In her autobiographical account, Bem (1998) describes herself and her then husband as truly egalitarian partners and parents who went to great lengths to bring up their children according to gender-liberated, anti-homophobic and sex-positive feminist ideals – in a very non-traditional gendered way, shielding them from as much gender stereotyping as possible. When she is an adult and being interviewed for the book, Emily, her daughter, says (1998: 198) that she has 'a serious doll and paper-doll collection and a collection of tea cups for tea parties' – all very girly. 'I have always played with costumes and clothing but I also played soccer, softball, and field hockey until my interest in theatre finally took over'. Emily's brother, Jeremy, states (1998: 180) that his intellectual interests are 'maths, computer programming and physics', but asserts that this is because he is good at them, not as a result of him being male. As adults, both Emily and Jeremy have very liberal views in relation to sexuality and gender expression. It is, however, interesting to note that although both children were brought up in as non-gendered a way as is conceivably possible within Western society, they both ended up with interests that fit their gender stereotypes. Is this coincidence? A reaction to their unusual upbringing or biology? There is, of course, no simple answer.

Reflective questions

If you are a parent or if you work with children, have you noticed girls and boys playing in gendered ways? Do you have any reaction to this?

5. Groups

Example 5.1

In the garden in summer, two boys and three girls were playing together. They took it in turns to lie face down on the grass, while one of the other children tickled, prodded or stroked their arms, legs or backs with a variety of natural objects such as leaves, sticks, stones, feathers and so on. The child then had to guess what the object was that was being used and who was using it.

Example 5.2

A group of children – four girls and four boys, with an age range of four to ten – were playing in an empty field on a camp site. The oldest children were girls and they seemed to direct operations, although every child seemed equally free to voice their opinions regarding what to play. They began by all individually doing gymnastics – cartwheels and handstands for a while and then began to play 'footie' for over an hour with lots of laughter and shrieking. The older girls monitored both rule-breaking and rule-making, but occasionally had the final say which the others accepted. They then all sat down on the grass – the girls spontaneously started braiding each other's hair and picking daisies, while the boys threw stones at a target, but the whole group remained in conversation reliving a common experience from the previous day involving 'capturing' a stationary tractor and planning their next adventure.

Example 5.3

Two older boys (10–11) had earlier erected a rope and tyre swing on a school playing field. A younger (7–9) mixed group came to play on it and before long had established that to be fair they would all queue and everyone would have a go at pushing and everyone would get a turn on the swing, while the rest of the group loudly chanted to twenty. All was going well until a boy of similar age ran over and jumped the queue, grabbing the swing. All the other children warily protested and told him to get off and take his turn, but he refused. The 'pusher' then suggested to the group that no-one pushed him to which they all agreed. There was a brief stand-off and then the boy on the swing got off and moved away, while the group noisily resumed their game with a 'whoop'.

We have observed plenty of examples of children playing in segregated groups and plenty where these groups are goading each other – usually, but not always consensually, but we included the above examples here because they were mixed groups with a varied age range. Interestingly they are all outside in natural environments. Perhaps such outdoor environments are less gendered and with only natural things and loose parts, they are also less gender-prescriptive, leaving children freer to play with each other. We have certainly noticed over time that when the props that are available for children to play with carry no obvious gender messages (which cannot be said of most toys), both sexes are more likely to explore these and play together. In Example 5.2, the group ended up doing stereotypically different things (hair-braiding and stone-throwing), but still remained together in a lively democratic conversation celebrating their joint escapades.

6. Friendships

Example 6.1

Siblings, aged seven (girl) and nine (boy), go to a mixed-sex school, but do not play out in their neighbourhood, so mainly choose their friends from school. The girl had friends of both sexes, mainly girls, but invited both boys and girls back to her house for tea or to play. She played both traditionally male and female-type games. The boy was only friendly with boys and was only prepared to play with girls if they played table tennis, football or golf. Two years later, the girl now only has friends of her own sex and plays more 'girly' things, although she still loves to play outdoors at physically challenging things. The boy is still only friendly with boys and remains interested in sports.

Example 6.2

A boy was approaching his sixth birthday and his mother asked him which friends he wanted to invite to his party. He said that he only wanted boys and reeled off a list of names, including the name of one girl. His mother pointed out that he had said he only wanted boys and the boy replied: 'She doesn't count. She plays like a boy.'

Example 6.3

Ali got chatting in a café to a nine-year-old girl who lives in a small coastal hamlet and attends a primary school of 120 children. When asked if she had friends and where she played when she wasn't at school, she said, 'my friends are all girls and we go to each other's houses. I do sometimes talk to boys at school but I never play with them' – at which point she pulled a face showing disgust.

Examples 6.1 and 6.2 show girls voluntarily playing with boys and 'playing like boys'. This is not always the case – as in Example 6.3 – but it is far more frequent in all the research that we have seen than boys adapting to or 'playing like girls' although we have seen and collected stories of boys who will individually play with a girl when there are no other children about. Peer pressure clearly has a contribution to make here. Children will play with children of the opposite sex if the context is right, as examples 5.1 to 5.3 show, but in more instances than not, as the children grow older, these friendships often die out when the circumstances change and/or puberty occurs. On the whole, children elect to befriend and play with others of their own sex and this has been noted in research across a wide-range of societies.

Play partners

Children's preference to play with others of their own sex has been extensively documented (Maccoby [2003], Whiting and Edwards [1988], Smith [2010], Lippa [2005], Thorne [1993/2009], Kane [2013]). Girls apparently tend to initiate this at around three years of age and boys soon after also reinforce it, with both girls and boys showing strong preferences and avoidances. It is most marked in nursery or school settings, when there are more children of both sexes; in the home or neighbourhood, in which the choice may be smaller or non-existent, children will sometimes opt to play with members of the opposite sex. Eliot (2010) gives examples from studies where it has been found that girls with older brothers play more sport and boys with twin sisters are more verbal that boys with twin brothers. Context clearly plays a role in gender matters.

Example 7.1

A seven-year-old boy has a girl as his best friend. His mother recounted that when she came to play the two children played differently to when the boy played with his friends who were boys. When the boys came to play, they tended to play with police, fire and army toys. When the girl came to play, they play more imaginative role-play games, making mischief, being detectives and so on. The boy said that when he played with the girl at school playtime, they just wandered around talking (behaviour usually associated with girl play) and when he played with the boys, they rushed about (behaviour usually associated with boy play). He stated that he played 50/50 with the boys and the girl, but his mother believed that he preferred playing with the girl.

We all have group and individual identities and this is also true of playing children, who may also have many identities with different gender biases, depending on whom they are with and where they are at any one time. For any child seeking play partners, their family composition and culture, the availability of friends of either sex and their own personality traits in terms of shyness and/or taking initiative, will all play a part in who they befriend.

Reflective questions

What are your own memories of playing? Who did you play with at what? How 'gendered' was your playing?

Gender segregation

Children do sometimes cross the gender divide – but in groups they do this rarely and not always successfully, as other children can make it clear that they have 'transgressed'. It is much easier for girls to cross into the boys' world than for boys to cross into the girls', as we can see from some of the examples above and the one following.

Example 8.1

Two boys, aged five and six, were playing in a pub garden. They had found sticks and were brandishing them firstly in mock battle and then latterly as wands. A girl of similar age, whose parents were absorbed in chatting to the boys' parents, tried on a few occasions to join in with the boys' game – she ran with them and imitated them, but they took no notice of her. After a while, she gave up and went back to the parents' table and hunted around in a bag. She brought out a pink plastic toy hairdryer, looked at it thoughtfully and then darted back to the boys where she jumped in front of them in true superhero style, pointed her hairdryer at the ground with a flourish and announced 'this is a fix-it machine!' Both boys stopped and looked impressed. 'What can it fix?' asked one to which the girl said triumphantly, 'whatever you want!' and for the next fifteen minutes the three children roared around together creating characters and problems for the machine to fix.

David Walliams' (2010) book, *The Boy in the Dress*, explores gender identity and gender non-conformity in an amusing and quite subtle way; it ends with a whole football team of boys who play and win a tournament, while wearing dresses. In real life, things are not always so easy for children who sometimes want to be gender non-conforming, unless they are super-confident and it is clearly harder for boys. 'Tomboys' are acknowledged and often accepted, but their male equivalents are called 'cissies' (even by researchers) and are often not tolerated – to a greater or lesser degree – by parents, adults or other children. Although Eliot (2010) tells us that nearly a quarter of her research cohort of boys experimented in cross-sex behaviour, dressing up in women's clothes being one of these, this was almost exclusively when alone and not in the public domain.

Example 8.2

A boy, aged nine, and a bit of a joker when he is feeling comfortable with the company, was at a family party at which 'Britain's Got Talent' was being played and he was singing and dancing 'Gangnam style' with his uncle. In order to entertain, he first wore his sister's pale blue leotard with track suit trousers over it and then at a suitable juncture in the singing and dancing, he bobbed behind a cupboard and reappeared wearing a multi-coloured frizzy wig and a pale blue tutu in place of the trousers. His uncle lifted him up and twirled him around a bit. It was very funny and everybody laughed a lot. His mother said that he wouldn't want his friends to know, because they might laugh at him.

Example 8.3

At an adventure playground, where male and female dressing-up clothes are available, the boys and girls sometimes come together to dress-up in the same sorts of clothes. The boys particularly love putting on women's clothes, jewellery, make-up and wigs and mincing around with handbags over their shoulders. They laugh a lot to show that this is done for a giggle, and not for real.

Example 8.4

A boy and a girl, both aged six and only children of parents who were close friends, used to stay over regularly at each other's houses. When they were together, they reportedly played differently from how they played either alone or when with friends of the same sex. On one occasion, the two of them spent two hours playing with fans and making up dances to ethereal songs. The boy really got into the whole thing, swirling and whirling with his fan.

We can see from the examples 8.2 to 8.4, and also from some of the previous examples, that boys are comfortable to cross the gender-divide, if they feel safe to express themselves in ways that are considered to be female, but only in particular contexts, i.e. in playful situations when the people or person they are with are accepting; when they feel confident about their own gender expression; when they do not fear being ridiculed, but feel in charge of their own game. Some boys never have this opportunity because it is not acceptable to their parents, carers or local peer group. There is usually very little fuss made if a girl wants to dress or act as for instance, a pirate or cowboy, when they are playing, although some parents and carers may even try to deter them from this because they see their daughter as 'their little princess'.

An interesting finding of the detailed observations by Blatchford et al. (2003) was that boys aged seven to eight, engaged in fantasy play more often than girls did, but their fantasy play involved more physical activity.

Boys and girls do sometimes test the boundaries between them and come together. Thorne (1993: 64) has termed this 'borderwork', sometimes reducing the sense of difference but often strengthening the codes of each gender group. Maccoby (2003: 67) gives some examples of the sorts of provocations that occur between groups of girls and boys, such as 'you can't get me!' and then a chase ensues. 'If a girl catches a boy, the ritual usually calls for the girls to kiss the boy triumphantly, with applause from other girls and taunts from other boys.' This is meant as a form of insulting, demeaning of, contaminating the boy. Maccoby also suggests that as children get older, cross-sex contacts are often seen in sexual or romantic terms and children

FIGURE 3.2 *Will girls be girly?*
Permission granted by Hope, Ferrante and Peach

can get teased for liking or loving the other child. We have certainly seen this regularly borne out in school playgrounds and classrooms between ten and eleven-year olds, especially in their last months at primary school.

Thorne (1993: 65) suggests that when gender boundaries are activated, boys and girls become 'The Boys' and 'The Girls', thereby heightening the awareness of how different the two groups are. This is sometimes emphasized by adults who organize games and activities pitting the sexes against each other. Thorne suggests that confident and high-status boys, who are well regarded by their male peer group, are more likely than less confident or well regarded boys, to join in girls' games without fear of ridicule. Eliot (2010) and Smith (2010) think that 'separation is a fact of human childhood. As long as there are enough kids to form a group, the first split will be down gender lines'. Maccoby (2003: 187) says that *sex-segregation* is so universal, that girls and boys are spending much of their childhood in 'separate gendered cultures with their own dynamics, rules and understandings, which impacts on their future relationships with one another in the home'. Maccoby feels that boy-culture and girl-culture are so different that she describes them as living in two separate worlds which have a significant effect on the way that girls and boys interact when they 'collide during adolescence', for instance, girls being much more adept and comfortable with intimacy than boys. 'Two-world theory' has of course become popularized with the notion that women are 'from Venus' and men are 'from Mars' and there are a number of self-help books available now for parents with advice and suggestions on combatting girl-culture and boy-culture and raising their children's awareness of gender stereotypes and the harm they can cause e.g. Brown (2014) and Eliot (2010).

Thorne (2009: 106) on the other hand acknowledges sex-segregation, but is not comfortable with this notion of two different cultures as she considers that research shows as much 'in-gender variation' as 'between-gender variation' and also that any particular social interaction between boys and girls can be 'simultaneously cooperative and competitive, self-assertive and oriented to others, and brash and vulnerable' and that these qualities don't sharply divide by gender. Goodwin (2006: 16) concurs, giving multiple examples of girls seeking out conflict and excluding one another to explode the myth that 'boys are assertive and girls are prosocial'. As we have discussed before, different researchers can interpret the same information differently.

Reflective questions

Did you play primarily with your own sex? What memories do you have of playing with your opposite gender? When you are observing children play, do you see them segregating according to their gender?

Why boys and girls may choose own sex groups

There has been a range of reasons put forward as to why it is believed that girls and boys choose to play mainly in same sex groups; for instance:

- Play-styles preferences – i.e. choosing to play with those who want to play in the same way and the same types of play activity;

- Wanting to be included/liked and so conforming to what others want;

- Wanting to be accepted as a girl or a boy and so behaving as other girls or boys do;

- Group consolidation of gender identity and/or gender role;

- Cultural/familial expectations; or

- Hormonal urges.

Whatever the causes, voluntary sex-segregation in childhood seems to happen in every culture that has been studied, but it is by no means completely fixed and individual children can and do still play with their opposite sex at different times.

Reflective questions

How do you react to this? Does it bother you or not? Does it matter or not? As an adult, do you find yourself mainly socializing with people of your own sex, or are you equally comfortable being friendly with people of both sexes?

The views of some workers, volunteers and workshop attendees

We carried out a very small-scale informal survey of twenty qualified and volunteer playworkers who worked at adventure playgrounds and after-school clubs, further details of which are also included in Chapter 6. It included asking them whether they considered that boys and girls played differently and if they did, in what way? Of those asked, 75 per cent replied with an unequivocal 'yes' and the other 25 per cent said 'yes but', depending upon circumstances such as age, siblings and friendship groups. Differences that were mentioned include that: girls play in smaller groups; girls prefer arts and crafts; girls like making things; girls dress up and play schools; girls become princesses. Similarly, boys play with the tools and fight; boys are more boisterous and smash things; boys go outside more, play sports and rough and tumble; boys play at cowboys and indians; boys do dangerous things; boys play football and boys become superheroes. This is all describing gender stereotyped play that fits into what the researchers' findings suggest, despite the efforts on the part of the workers to ensure that there were no gender biases.

Reflective question

Should we be at all concerned about this?

A small group of girls on an adventure playground were asked the question about whether boys and girls played differently and replied very definitely that, yes, boys and girls played differently. However, when asked to give examples, there were only two differences that they could think of. One was that boys fight and the other was that when painting a large structure some girls used pink paint and none of the boys did or would!

Three boys, aged four, seven and eleven, were separately asked whether boys and girls played differently – all three boys cited girls as playing with Barbie and boys playing football and all three said they would never play with Barbie, but that girls do play football. The four year old was subsequently seen playing with Barbie with a girl of a similar age and clearly enjoying himself dressing one up and combing her hair, while chatting to his female playmate!

There is, of course, always an inherent danger in asking or interviewing people that they will give answers that seem wholly representative of their views at the time, but that in reality will be partial and inconsiderate of other contexts and experiences which are just not salient or obvious to them at the time of questioning. It is probably true for all of us that whenever we watch children playing, we watch with an unconscious gender filter that may prevent us from seeing and understanding the subtle differences, motives, feelings and social orders in children's play. Without a closer look and an open questioning of our own underlying beliefs, we may be making all kinds of assumptions.

Gendered toys and games

Toys and games appear to be even more gendered now than they ever were in the days when gender discrimination was the norm. Prior to the 1970s, there always had been toys specifically for boys and girls based on gender stereotypes, i.e. girls had domestic, arts and crafts and nurturing based toys and boys had construction, action and wheeled based toys but there was not the rigid segregation by colour and fantasy-based characters (pink princess or blue action hero), that there seems to be now. The 1970s produced far more gender-neutral toys as feminism was at its height, but, as time has gone on, these seem to be a thing of the past. Even such things as bicycles and balls now come in pink for girls and blue for boys – certainly clever marketing, as this means that the toy makers can sell even more items but does it actually affect the being and becoming of our boys and girls? Toddlers will play with anything regardless of whatever colour or character association it has, but as children get older, the media and peer pressure exert their influence and children who are prey to this start wanting things associated with their own gender. Does this matter? There are certainly some researchers who would say yes, and some who would say no. Play and child development psychologist, A. Gummer, in Barford (2014) thinks a 'healthy play diet' is important, so that children have choices across the spectrum of play whether they are pink, blue or neither.

There are no definitive answers. We know that given the opportunities, children love to play with loose parts which are not gender-prescriptive; natural loose parts such as stones, cones, sticks, shells, leaves, twigs, water, sand, mud, etc. and those that are manmade such as tyres, bricks, rope, string, paper, boxes, jars, blankets and so on. We have observed time and again how all children imaginatively engage with these loose parts and how these can enhance children's development and can foster non-segregated play, but we are not aware of any formal research about whether boys and girls play differently with loose parts or what the longer term consequences might be of such play in terms of their gender expression.

Reflective questions

What do you think? Are gendered toys causing girls and boys to play in even more gendered ways than they did before and might this indirectly support ongoing inequality between males and females in our society? Or do you think that boys and girls play differently regardless of what they play with?

Are there really innate differences between the ways that boys and girls play and what they play with or are all differences socially constructed? There are certainly many researchers who would say yes, there are differences, and many more who would say yes with the reservation that it is society that causes this to happen and not a natural inclination on the part of boys and girls, and there are others who consider that there are very few or even no differences, because they have never come across them. It is interesting to note that all the people to whom we spoke, who are concerned about the causes of any perceived differences between the ways that boys and girls play, found it very difficult to say that they have seen differences, without referring to what they consider to be the causes of this i.e. gender socialization.

Reflective questions

Do you think it is important to think about the reasons as to why there may or may not be differences between the play behaviours of boys and girls? Do you think that believing certain things would alter the way that you look at girls and boys playing and if so, what effect do you think this would have?

In this chapter we have looked at a few examples of what we and others have observed when boys and girls play and we have recorded anecdotal evidence as well as talking to a few children about this. What can we conclude from this? We can see from formal research and from our own more informal questioning that it is impossible to say unequivocally that boys and girls play the same or differently, but that many of our observations do show some examples of stereotypical gendered play behaviour. Of course, there are similarities but there are also some differences between the way that boys and girls play, and, or the perception of how they play. Whether this is true, what might cause such differences and whether these might be significant in terms of their lives as a whole is explored further in the following chapters.

Suggested reading

Fine, C. (2011), *Delusions of Gender*, London: Icon Books.
Smith, P. (2010), *Children and Play*, Oxford: Wiley-Blackwell.
Thorne, B. (1993/2009), *Gender Play – Girls and Boys in School*, Maidenhead: Open University Press.
Walliams, D. (2010), *The Boy in the Dress*, London: HarperCollins.

CHAPTER FOUR

The theoretical perspective

Introduction

This chapter will explore the varying theories which try to explain why there may be differences between the interests and play behaviours of, and within the groups labelled as, boys and girls. It will outline theories that are formed by research undertaken within the spheres of biology, education, psychology and sociology and will examine the biases within each and search for those that appear more conclusive (if indeed there are any). There is no one proven theory to explain how or why children either acquire or perform their gender roles and gender identities. All theories are speculative.

In previous chapters, we have explored what has led us to the current interest in sex and gender and we have given anecdotal and observed evidence of boys and girls playing. In this chapter, we shall look at some of, what are considered to be the main differences between men and women/boys and girls and the multiplicity of research, carried out by a range of scientists, that is done to find out about these supposed differences and we will examine what influences are brought to bear on children that may cause these differences. We will also consider the potential predispositions that might affect the judgement of those scientists carrying out their research. The brain is not like a jigsaw that is worked on until it is complete. Scientists are discovering that the brain is continually changing in line with its current circumstances and it would therefore be inappropriate to think that children are the only people whose behaviours are influenced by external and internal experience and hormonal activity.

We will begin by looking at the controversial battlefield that constitutes the perceived similarities and differences between males and females. We use the term 'battlefield' because there is a plethora of literature on the subject with many authors arguing from different perspectives and quoting scientific evidence to support their case that is often hotly belied by other authors. There seems to be huge emotional investment and interest in either proving or disproving gender differences. Many books sound extremely plausible and highly knowledgeable – we have found ourselves agreeing with volumes as we read them that ended up completely contradicting each other and recognized early on that we needed to sit back and weigh the 'evidence' carefully. Exactly a century ago (have we made so little progress?), Woolley (1914: 372) found the same problem:

> The general discussions of the psychology of sex, whether by psychologists or by sociologists show such a wide diversity of points of view that one feels that the truest thing to be said at present is that scientific evidence plays very little part in producing convictions.

More recently Lippa (2005) suggests that 'gender is (still) a hot topic' amongst scientists and indeed Cealy-Harrison and Hood-Williams (2002: 145) put this very succinctly when they suggest:

> We might say of research into the differences between sexes that it tells us more about the social, political and intellectual concerns that animate it than about the difference between boys and girls.

This problem has also been highlighted by Thorne (1993/2009) in that she thinks that researchers in educational settings tend to be blind to children's play that deviates from 'typical gender norms' and she feels that they do not notice variations within gender groups. Anggard (2011: 7) agrees and suggests that gender should be seen as 'situated, temporary and flexible discursive constellations' rather than two separate and oppositional aspects of self.

Many authors state, as does Lippa (2005: xiv), that they are going to offer 'a balanced and fair-minded account of what science currently does and does not know about the behaviour of males and females', although one can often detect a bias of some sort. Others, such as Jordan-Young (2011), are distinctly unhappy about particular areas of research; she particularly pours scorn on Brain Organization Theory. She does not appear to try to give a balanced account but spends her energies disproving the findings of many neuroscientists.

Let us be clear here, we are not scientists, we have no reason to support one theory or another, but we are interested in how views on gender differences affect the way that people support children's play and therefore we are going to try to be balanced by giving examples of a range of theories from different areas of research for you to ponder. We will leave you to decide whether any of them 'speak' to you in a way that informs or confirms your own thinking and the way that you think about the behaviour of girls and boys and indeed how you behave with them.

Theories about gender

There are many ways that theories about gender differences can be grouped. For instance, Lippa (2005) suggests that theories about gender focus on these four kinds of explanations:

● Group level factors, such as the biological and social groups we belong to: These theories are all about the desire to belong and be like other people. Biological groups include members of our immediate family and people of the same gender, and social groups are our friends and people who attend the same social settings such as uniformed groups, youth clubs, after school setting and so on.

● Past biological and social-environmental factors, such as foetal hormones and parental rearing: these theories put a lot of emphasis on pre-birth hormonal effects, some of which are genetic and some which are determined by the mother's health and well-being and on the way that a child is reared within the family.

● Current biological and social-environmental factors, such as current hormone levels and social settings: these theories are all about what is happening to the child in the here and now. What hormones are being activated and what sort of social scene is the child involved in?

● Internal factors, such as personality traits, attitudes, stereotypes, and schemas: these theories are all about the makeup of the child herself or himself. What is her personality like? How does she feel about being a girl? What is her understanding of being a girl and so on?

We have previously suggested (Kilvington and Wood, 2010) that theories can be roughly grouped into those with a socio-cultural, external basis and based on nurture and those with a biological, internal basis and based on nature. In hindsight, these may seem a little over simplistic and pandering to an oppositional or binary view of how gender is 'done', but nevertheless they still represent many of the historical and current approaches taken to the study of sex and gender. They are as follows:

(a) **Nurture**

● Social Structure theories suggest that there are many different cultural contexts and all people are products of social construction. Gender is just part of this and society supports the different social positions that gender roles ascribe to.

● Social Role Theory tries to understand the stereotyped roles that men and women play and why there is this division of labour in different societies. It questions whether males and females are equally suited to all roles.

● Social Learning Theory suggests that children develop their gender identity and roles through a learning process that involves modelling, imitation and reinforcement of role models of the same sex. Children observe the behaviours of men and women, copy it, and then receive positive or negative responses to their own gendered behaviour, which in turn reinforces the development of gender roles.

● Social Cognitive Theory asserts that children are active participants in the process of socialization and their cognitive abilities are important in this. Children construct their own abstract models of both female and male-appropriate behaviour based on their observations and then adopt behaviour that fits their model. This may not be in line with, for instance, their relatives behaviour, so a girl may not imitate her mother, or a boy his older brother.

● Group Socialization Theory argues that peers are the most influential mediators and interpreters of gender. Rich-Harris (1999) suggests that children are socialized mainly by identifying with their peer group and then taking on that group's norms for attitudes and behaviours, including those associated with gender.

● Cognitive Development Theory proposes that gender cannot be learned until a child reaches a particular stage of intellectual development. According to this theory once the child has categorized her/himself as definitely being either a boy or a girl it will become a self-defining category.

● Gender Schema or Enculturated-Lens Theory, developed by Bem in the early 1980s, refers to the theory that children learn about what it means to be male and female from the culture in which they live. According to this theory, children adjust their behaviour to fit in with the gender norms and expectations of their culture. She felt that if all children were brought up in a 'gender-aschematic' culture, they would learn nothing about being male or female, would therefore not display any stereotypically male or female behaviour and therefore our culture would cease to be gendered.

(b) Nature

- Biological Theories stress the biological basis of gender difference. These purport that differences are the result of genetics – genes and chromosomes, which cause differences in reproductive parts, hormones, brain structure and brain chemistry and therefore the behaviour of males and females, and is all part of the evolutionary process. Neuroscientists are finding new information about the brain all the time and they certainly find many differences between the brains of males and females at all ages. Whether these differences are caused by genes, hormones or experiences is not agreed on. However Eliot (2010: 6) states that the 'brain actually changes in response to its own experiences [...] and in childhood the brain is far more plastic and malleable that at any other time – 'wiring itself in large measure according to the experiences in which it is immersed from prenatal life through adolescence – your brain is what you do with it'.

- Socio-Biological Theory supports the evolutionary theory too and is based on natural selection. It looks for evidence that links the social behaviour of animals and humans and suggests that males and females have developed different strategies of sexual selection and reproduction and this leads to differently gendered behaviour.

- Psychoanalytic Theory was instigated by Freud. It is the first theory of human personality to assign a central role to sexuality. This theory is based on the idea that behaviour (and therefore development) is influenced by our feelings and thoughts, many of which are unconscious and due to previous experiences.

- Essentialism is a theory whose proponents believe that certain properties possessed by a group are universal, and not dependent on context. For example 'women are more empathetic than men' is an essentialist statement based on the idea that gender differences in males and females can be attributed to (stereotypical gender) qualities possessed by males and females.

More recently, however, we have come up with a simpler way of categorizing all the expressed views about sex differences and these are shown in Table 1.

Table 1. Categories of expressed views about sex differences

Category A	Category B	Category C	Category D
Those who believe there are many and varied definite differences between boys and girls. They believe that some of these differences are 'hard-wired' at birth due to hormonal and chromosomal action and that we do both boys and girls a disservice if we do not recognize these and shape our personal responses and our educational, medical and social services accordingly.	Those who believe there are just a very few genuine innate differences between girls and boys, that are often compounded and exacerbated by societal expectations and which can be minimized if understood. They believe that men and women are far more alike than dissimilar and that within-gender variation is much greater than between-gender variation.	Those who believe there are no proven differences at all between the sexes apart from basic physiology and that any apparent differences are all socially constructed. They believe that claims of biological differences are down to poor and biased research.	Those who believe there probably are differences, but rather than try to prove the causes, they concentrate on recognizing and responding to children who are grappling with these in the here and now.
Proponents include: Brizendine (2007, 2010), Sax (2005), Gurian (2011), Tannen (1990), Moir and Jessel (1991), Baron-Cohen (2004) and Biddulph (1998, 2013).	Proponents include: Pfaff (2011), Maccoby (2003), Lippa (2005), Shibley-Hyde (2005) Eliot (2010) and Brown (2014).	Proponents include: Jordan-Young (2010), Fine (2011), Bem (1998) and Fausto-Sterling (2000).	This category includes: Katch (2001), Paley (1984), Martin (2011) and Holland (2003).

A t this point, which category seems to sum up what you believe?

Proponents of Category A tell us that in the pursuit for equality between women and men during the sixties, seventies and eighties, western society believed – or was encouraged to believe – that all women and men were essentially the same in terms of their abilities and capabilities and that it was sexist to think otherwise. This made sense at the time of course because the higher cause of equality was too politically important to seriously question and professionals and public alike did not want to be guilty of sexual prejudice. However, as we moved into the 1990s, some scientific researchers were beginning to publicly contest the idea and presenting papers that appeared to show that differences between the average man and woman did exist after all. Contributions from the emerging field of neuroscience also began to line up and before long there was an explosion of books declaring there were proven differences between men and women in the ways they thought, communicated and behaved that were rooted in biology. Many of these books were best-sellers and appealed to a 'societal common sense' – we always 'knew' deep down that we were different, but now it was possible to be both different and equal.

'The nature and cause of brain differences are now known beyond specu-lation, beyond prejudice and beyond reasonable doubt' Moir and Jessel stated (1991: 11) and claims were made by many authors for an astonishing array of variations. We list those that were most widely accepted:

- Females had more acute hearing and a wider range of vision, natural empathy, learnt to talk and to read more easily; were more concerned with people than things, preferred to socialize in pairs or small groups, like to question, make connections and see the wider picture, seek intimacy.

- Males were more physically active, more spatially aware, had greater mathematical and geometrical reasoning, were more competitive and displayed more aggression, prefer to be part of a bigger group, like to make rules and solve problems, are action-focussed and independent.

To be fair, early neuroscientists were conducting brain scans that did indeed show many differences between the sexes, but it took a few more years of research before an appreciation of the plasticity of the brain helped us all understand that our experiences throughout childhood and adulthood continue to shape our brains. As Eliot (2010: 6) says:

considering the very different ways boys and girls spend their time while growing up, as well as the special potency of early experience in moulding neuronal connections, it would be shocking if the two sexes' brains didn't work differently by the time they were adults.

This meant that research began to focus on newborns and young children in an attempt to find out whether some sex differences were 'hard-wired' and that girls and boys really are born with contrasting deviations, as opposed to developing these through social and environmental influences. The nature–nurture debate was still on!

Authors in Category B looked more critically at research that had been done and in the early noughties, 'studies of studies' and meta-analyses (a statistical method for aggregating research findings across many studies of the same question) were conducted that began to dilute and refute earlier claims and eliminate some of the bias in previous hypotheses. One tome (Ellis et al. 2008) summarized more than a century of research into the possible sex differences in the following areas:

- Basic biological factors
- The brain and biochemistry
- Health and illness factors
- Perceptual, motor and emotional factors
- Intellectual, cognitive, self-concept and mental health/illness factors
- Preferences, interests, attitudes, beliefs and intentions
- Responses to drugs, stress and therapeutics
- Personality and general behaviour
- Social behaviour
- Consuming and individual institutional interactions
- Stratification and work-related behaviour
- Attitudes and beliefs surrounding gender, physiological and cognitive responses to others based on sex, social treatment by others, victimization and portrayals in the mass media.

This work tabled approximately 18,000 studies, citing up to 30,000 sex differences that were either written in or translated into English (so there will be some omissions) and is a valuable reference resource. In their grand summary, Ellis et al. (2008: 941) list those differences where there were at least ten studies with corroborating evidence and conclude that these can be 'specified with a high degree of certainty' but also recognize that 'scientists continue to collect new evidence and in doing so, may eventually unearth exceptions or at least qualifications to what has been determined so far'. These 'most certain universal sex differences' (2008: 938) – many of which may be unsurprising are:

- Males are heavier at birth
- Males are taller following late adolescence
- Males have greater physical strength
- Males have a larger 2D:4D finger ratio
- Females have greater joint laxity
- Males have a larger head circumference and cranial capacity
- Females have higher leptin levels
- Females have higher rates of breast cancer
- Males experience a first heart attack at a younger age
- More females contract lupus
- Females have more headaches in general
- Females estimate/perceive greater hazards and injury risks in their environments
- Females have more stress/worry/anxiety associated with providing care to others
- Males are more prone to boredom
- Females cry more as adults

You may well feel somewhat deflated by these or on the contrary you may feel intrigued by some. Whatever your reaction, none of these findings tell us why these differences exist although certainly for some, Ellis et al. (2008: 941) and others say that 'differences that are truly universal would be virtually impossible to explain solely in terms of social training and cultural traditions. Some underlying biology must be in operation'.

Shibley-Hyde published her 'Gender Similarities Hypothesis' in 2005 in which she states that extensive evidence from meta-analyses show that males and females are alike on almost all psychological variables. There are a few notable exceptions that show large sex differences such as some motor behaviours (e.g. throwing distance) and some aspects of sexuality and aggression shows a moderate sex difference. Shibley-Hyde concludes that:

> it is time to consider the costs of overinflated claims of gender differences. Arguably, they cause harm in numerous realms, including women's

opportunities in the workplace, couple conflict and communication, and analyses of self-esteem problems among adolescents. Most important, these claims are not consistent with the scientific data. (2005: 590)

Neuroscientist Eliot – a specialist in plasticity – is emphatic that those in Category A have all concentrated on the extremes of differences rather than similarities and so make unauthentic and stereotypical claims. She asserts that overall there are only two proven facts: i) boys' brains are larger than girls, and ii) girls' brains and bodies, stop growing a year or two before boys, and that there are only 'a few truly innate differences between the sexes; in maturation rate, sensory processing, activity level, fussiness and play interests' (2010: 6). In very young children, as opposed to older children and adults, it seems she considers, there are very few differences in girls' and boys' brains.

Category C, too, includes neuroscientists who have also sieved through research evidence, but they conclude that much of the 'evidence' is 'premature speculation' (Fine 2011: 142) and that the interplay of brain, hormones, genes and environment – Lippa's 'causal thickets' – are actually far too complex to really draw any genuine conclusions about sex differences. Their argument is that we are so enmeshed in a range of genderized cultures and attitudes that it is incredibly difficult to be truly objective – whenever gender comes to the fore (becomes salient) in a situation or conversation, then we will react according to previously imprinted patterns of thinking and feeling often without even knowing. Fine argues that neuroscience is being used to reinforce old-fashioned stereotypes with all the 'authority' of science and would be better termed 'neurosexism', when the reality is that the constant interaction between the biological and the social, means that 'components of our political, social and moral struggles become, quite literally, embodied, incorporated into our very physiological being' (Fausto-Sterling 2000: 5).

Where does all this leave us? Do you find yourself warming to a particular category or do they all seem possible?! We find ourselves agreeing with Lippa (2005: 226) that 'rather than developing a universal theory of gender and honing in on one single answer to the nature-nurture questions, researchers may instead need to be satisfied with multiple theories and multiple answers. They may come to learn that different causal cascades lead to gender in different ways, in different groups, at different stages of life'. So in answer to where this now leaves us, perhaps it leaves us needing to explore Category D, for it is beyond both our expertise and the purpose of this book to resolve the arguments put forward in the other categories. We will return to this but first let us look at some of the research undertaken to try and prove or disprove these theories.

Fields of research into gender differences

So what of the research that has been undertaken that enables scientists to come up with their theories as above? Is Cealy-Harrison and Hood-Williams notion that research findings are influenced by a range of subjective ideas borne out by what we have found in our literature research? Let us start by looking at the range of fields of science that spawn research in the area of sex and gender differences. They fall mainly, but not exclusively within the social and biological sciences. The list below is long and incomplete, but does show the breadth of interest in the scientific world and therefore leads one to believe that the scientific basis of sex and gender differences in males and females must be considered to be important.

Psychology, developmental psychopathology, social psychology, developmental psychopathology, feminist psychology, evolutionary psychology, gender studies, psychiatry, neuro-psychiatry, genetic psychiatry, family therapy, sociology, socio-linguistics, linguistics, social philosophy, socio-medical, pharmacology, medicine, paediatrics, investigative journalism, computer science, education, early years development, biology, biological anthropology, anthropology, molecular biology, evolutionary biology, neurobiology, neuro-genetics, neuro-anatomy, behavioural neuro-science, neuro-physiology, endocrinology, behavioural-endocrinology, genetics, primatology, zoology, ethnology, pharmacology, physiology, urban geography – there may be more!

Reflective question

Why do you think so many scientists from these areas of research are interested in whether there are or are not differences, other than physical, in the behaviour of males and females?

Reasons for carrying out research into gender differences

Why do so many scientists want to do research in the field of sex differences? Lippa (2005) suggests that the debate about the causes of sex and gender differences is relevant to many public policy issues such as: same sex schooling; gender equity in schools; sexual coercion and violence; sexualization of childhood; the digital divide; equality in the workplace and so on. Becker et al. (2008) do not try to explain the causes of sex differences; they present another gigantic meta-analysis, from across the world, one that uses a 'vote counting method' and in the end come up with what they call 'irrefutable, universal sex differences in humans' and finally identify only traits for which there were at least 10 studies with no contradictory evidence. They see the results in terms of the future health and well-being of men and women across the world. Pfaff (2011) adds that he also sees sex differences as relating to sports, war and business.

For some, the study of sex differences is relevant in order to try and improve the lot of boys or girls (e.g. Sax [2006], Biddulph [1998, 2013], Brizendine [2007, 2010]). There are others who study sex differences in order to try and disprove that there are any, as they possibly believe that proving that there are differences between men and women, girls and boys perpetuates inequality between the sexes (see Butler [1990], Walkerdine [2004], Bem [1983]). Yet others see that understanding differences will help for therapeutic reasons and some see that the design of public spaces should include the play needs of boys and girls, who they perceive as having different needs. We believe that reflection on sex and gender differences is vital for people who work on behalf of children's play, because, as you will have seen in Chapter 3, the ways in which children play appear to be one of the areas where the largest differences have been observed by researchers. Those of us within the children's workforce may consider that these differences:

a) perpetuate any number of inequalities; or

b) that they are merely a free expression of boys and girls at play; or

c) that their different behaviours are vital to their ongoing development of self.

We will return to the theme of how adults respond to potential differences in children's gendered play, in Chapter 6, but meanwhile consider the following questions. Is it possible that our behaviour is not influenced by our views? That we are able to take an objective stance? Surely our views inform our practice?

Research in the field of neuroscience and biology

What sort of research do these scientists do in relation to differences in males and females? We have mentioned meta-analysis above, but clearly, in most cases, it depends upon which areas of science they are involved with as to what sort of research they do. We can only show a small sample of research here in order to give a flavour of this. So for instance, those in the field of neuroscience, whose interest is mainly in the anatomy and function of the brain, use mainly techniques from the fields of chemistry, physiology and anatomy, including post-mortem studies on areas of the brain. An example of this is that they carry out controlled experiments on male and female animals with the addition of certain amounts of chemicals usually produced by the action of the brain of either males or females, and then observe the behaviour to see if it has become more typical of the male or female animal. This is, sometimes equated to the behaviour of humans. As an example of this Pfaff (2011: 35) says that neuro-anatomists from Kansas University who were interested in hormones, found after an initial experiment on guinea pigs, that the offspring of female rhesus monkeys that had been administered testosterone prenatally, 'showed more male-type sex behaviours, but were also masculinized in other aspects of behaviour. The most obvious one was an increased tendency to engage in rough and tumble play similar to normal males'. These findings concur with Baron-Cohen's team's findings from a longitudinal study that have reported associations between testosterone in amniotic fluid and some indicators of sex-typed interests, although according to Jordan-Young, these findings have not been replicated and are therefore not valid.

Pfaff (2011: 58) gives an example of sex differences in the structure of the basal forebrain of humans. He tells us that Dick Swaab, a medical doctor, and Roger Gorski, a neurobiologist, both studied brains of patients who had died. They found that the hypothalamic cell group is larger in males than in females. However, the age of the male affects the magnitude of the difference. From Swaab's research, it was found that these extra male neurons have an overload of sex hormone receptors. But Pfaff says that it is not known exactly how this plays out in human psychology, although we suspect it implies extra interest in sexual activity!

Neuroscientists, as do many scientists interested in sex and gender differences, study children with intersex syndromes, such as Congenital Adrenal Hyperplasia (CAH), a genetic disorder that causes overproduction of androgens (male sex hormones) from the adrenal glands. Babies born with this condition often have ambiguous genitalia and because of this, have a sex assigned to them, which is not necessarily their biological sex. Scientists compare their behaviour to that of siblings, relatives or other linked people without the condition. Jordan-Young (2011: 73) says that 'fourteen out of eighteen studies that examined aspects of play behaviour find that CAH girls are more masculine in at least some dimension.' However, she goes on to say that more robust studies, e.g. Berenbaum and Hines (1992), Pasterski et al. (2005), show that the CAH girls are only more likely to play with so-called boys' toys, such as building blocks or vehicles, rather than so called girls' toys, such as dolls or cooking implements. She found no other 'robust' evidence for consistent differences in any other aspects of play.

Brain Organization researchers also use a range of non-invasive brain imaging techniques in their controlled experiments on men and women to see if the brains of males and females function differently under the same conditions. They carry out, what Jordan-Young terms 'quasi experiments' which are uncontrolled because of their nature – e.g. the study of pre-natal hormones on the later behaviour, or sexuality of boys and girls. Psychologist Fine (2011) and Jordan-Young (2011) a socio-medical scientist, among others, consider, as suggested before, that most neuro-scientific findings are hopelessly flawed, partly because they think they come from an androcentric (historically male biased) perspective and also because of what might be termed 'cognitive dissonance', the inability to learn something new because of long-held inaccurate beliefs, those being, in their case, that there are natural differences between men and women's behaviour. They also believe that much neuro-scientific research is carried out agnotologically, intimating that the studies are also flawed because of ignorant cultural or ideological schemas that cause researchers to block certain information or fail to incorporate certain facts into their overall findings or thinking on a subject. Fine (2011: 134) talks of the so-called 'file-drawer phenomenon', whereby studies that do find sex differences get published, but those that don't, languish unpublished and unseen in a researcher's file drawer.

The neuro-biological approach to differences between males and females appears to support 'biological determinism' which diminishes human capacity for taking control of one's own life. Rather than being just a bundle of uncontrollable hormones, Carole Bead (1994: xvii) suggests that 'biology is not destiny and the fact that we can observe differences in how boys and girls behave does not mean that those differences are inevitable or unchangeable.' Pfaff (2011: 7) a neurobiologist/behaviourist, asks what the biological truth is behind widespread beliefs in differences between the male and female mind and goes on to say 'books written for the general public have not handled this subject well.' He says that sometimes the problem is exaggeration motivated by political affiliations. Pfaff (2011: 69) believes there are a few behavioural differences between men and women, but that these (and he cites five) are all related to the function of reproduction and result from genetic, hormonal and neuro-chemical influences. They are as follows:

- Sex behaviours

- Parental behaviours

- Aggression

- Friendly pro-social behaviours

- Responses to pain

Pfaff (2011: 85) does tell us that sexual behaviours in 'higher primates' (humans) are also 'strongly influenced by social context'.

Epigenetics

The way that we express our gender identity may be a result of epigenetic changes that occur in our development. Epigenetics is the study of changes in gene expression, caused by different bits of our DNA being turned on and off. It is believed that these changes have possibly resulted in our evolution from apes to human beings. Epigenetic changes can occur in different parts of our DNA – in our 'germline' or in our 'somatic cells'. It is thought that a host of internal and external variables, such as steroid hormones, endocrine disrupting chemicals, early child abuse or context dependent learning can cause these epigenetic changes, but the gene imprint that is created by this may only affect the person to whom the changes have occurred or may be passed on from generation to generation. However, from what is currently known it seems that some epigenetic changes are definitely hereditary and gender expression is considered to be possibly one of these. The study of epigenetics in relation to gender is still in its early stages and we could find no clear evidence of research relevant for this book. We did come across a paper by Joel Seth (2012: 24) in which he talks about epigenetics and says 'The environment we create, in which our children play and manoeuvre, will not only affect those children, but their children and their children's children.' Does this include their gender identity?

Research in the fields of social science

What of social science research? Fine (2011: 170) tells us that bioethicist Eric Racine and colleagues coined a new term 'neuro-realism', which describes how brain imaging can make psychological phenomena seem more real or objective because it uses complex machinery, is undertaken by technicians in white coats and shows 'pictures' of behaviour in the brain. It looks far more scientific for instance, if the pleasure-centre in the brain fires up an image on a screen when someone eats a doughnut, than if they tick a box on a questionnaire marked 'yes I really enjoyed eating that doughnut'! Fine worries that some scientists seem to equate 'actual nature' with 'brain' and she suggests that neuroscience outranks psychology in the implicit hierarchy of 'scientificness', in the minds of many. Neuroscientific explanations are more difficult for people to question and photographs of brain activation are very compelling.

Reflective question

What do you think about neuroscientific explanations?

Social scientists use a wide range of different research techniques when looking at potential differences between the behaviours of males and females including the following methods: exploratory research, comparative studies, surveys, cross-sectional and longitudinal studies, experimental and quasi-experimental research, case and pilot studies, meta-analysis, hypothesis testing, field research and so on. Interestingly, during the course of our extensive reading we have not come across any literature where neuroscientists have disputed the findings of sociologists or psychologists. However, Rosenthal (1963) wrote an article on the Social Psychology of the Psychological Experiment, that showed just how much a researchers expectations could influence the outcome of a study. Indeed, in their giant tome, *Sex Differences in the Brain: From Genes to Behaviour* (2008), Becker et al. (Professor of Psychology and Psychiatry working in a neuroscience department) did a meta-analysis of a wealth of varied research that had been undertaken on sex differences from across the world during the previous century and this included research from a plethora of different scientific backgrounds.

Multiple causes of gender

We believe that there are few current scientists who are not, at least, prepared to accept that gender differences probably have multiple causes. It is a question of degree as to which are considered the 'primary' causes, and it is the degree of influence that this primary cause exerts, which is the subject of the hot debates. Bead (1994: 6–11) suggests that there are three different ways in which children develop expressions of gender:

- Biological heritage – children brought up within a society in which biology and socialization interact.

- Punctuated socialization – learning gender comes at specific points in a child's development. It is not a smooth and continual but periodic process.

- Asymmetric socialization – it is easier for girls to be tomboys and do boy things than vice versa.

Eliot (2010: 136) says: 'Gender differences begin as little seeds, planted by genes and hormones but nurtured through social learning, gender identification and children's strong urges to conform.' Lippa (2005: 259) speaks of 'a complex cascade of biological and environmental factors' that result in gender.

As examples of social science research, sometimes both males and females are studied together and sometimes just one sex. For instance, the following two examples show how girls' and boys' friendships seem to be different, but this is taken from two studies that concentrated on one sex only.

Boys' friendships

Christine Skelton, Professor of Gender Equality in Education at the University of Birmingham, UK (2001) noted through her observations in primary schools that six- to seven-year-old boys formed large, loosely connected groups, with no particular tight friendship groups, but seemingly arranged in a somewhat hierarchical nature.

Girls' friendships

Mary Kehily, now Senior Lecturer in Childhood and Youth Studies at the Open University (2002) became an 'honorary' member of a group of eight- to nine-year-old girls who met regularly in a different school playground during breaks and discussed topics of mutual interest, such as friends, boys and puberty. With the girls' agreement, Kehily participated and recorded the conversations, some of which were of quite an intimate nature. Among other findings, Kehily and her colleagues proposed that the discourses that the girls engaged in demonstrated what it meant to be both a girl and a friend; they also noted that the girls appeared to feel very safe with each other.

Boys and girls together

Kane (2013: 111) tells us that Lisa Karsten, Professor of Urban Geography at the University of Amsterdam (2003) has studied playgrounds in the multicultural areas of Amsterdam and the broader pattern documented by this research was one of gender-segregated play in which boys' peer groups were larger and tended to dominate and control the physical space. However, she also reveals variations with some girls challenging traditional gender divides, especially when their female peer groups were particularly large.

Parental influence

Kane (2013: 59) also points to another style of research, related to the influences that possibly affect children's performance of gender, when she tells us that Krafchick et al. (2005) carried out content analysis on the best-selling parenting books in the USA. This revealed the message that mothers should

FIGURE 4.1 *Playing across the gender divide*
Permission granted by Doherty and Elliott

be the primary caregivers to children, boys are naturally more independent and girls more nurturing. The outcome of this content analysis would cause a shudder of horror in the minds of many social scientists and feminists alike!

Reflective questions

What do you think about the results of the content analysis of the parenting books? And indeed, the indirect gender messages in many children's books too?

Toy choice by gender

Jordan-Young (2011) gives us an interesting example of controlled observational research. She tells us that Servin et al. (2003) carried out a study of girls with CAH to determine their play preferences. They arranged toys that had been defined as masculine, feminine or neutral in a semi-circle and invited children, one at a time, to play with them. The results showed that although girls with CAH spent significantly more time with toys classed as masculine than did the control girls, but the most popular toy with all the girls was a toy coded as masculine!

Various experiments have been carried out on gender stereotypical play for boys and girls. Fine (2011) gives examples in her chapter on 'The Self Socializing Child' of how children can be influenced in their choice of toys or playing, by labelling or designing them as for a specific sex. For example, four-year-old children of both sexes played for three times longer with a xylophone and balloons when they were told that they were things meant for their own sex rather than for children of the other sex. Referencing another study by Leinbach et al. (1993), Fine tells us that researchers transformed a pastel 'My Little Pony', (usually soft and pretty and designed for girls) by shaving the mane, painting it black and adding pointy teeth. Boys and girls then decided it was a boys' toy and the boys wanted to get one.

Segregated gender play

Thorne (1993), in her book called *Gender Play*, gives an example of observational research on segregated gendered play. She tells us of contests between groups of boys and girls who have their own conventions, thereby strengthening the gender divide. She talks of these as 'rituals of pollution' whereby children of one sex (usually boys) are 'contaminated' by the touch of a child of the other sex (usually girls). She recounts one example when observing an older boy teaching a younger girl how to chase, while he shouted: 'Help – a girl's after me'.

Girls and boys play in natural outside places

Little research has been carried out on the construction of gender related to natural outdoor places. However, as Anggard (2011) says after a gender analysis of a multi-method study by Waller (2010) of children playing in a country park every week, 'the character of the nature environment can make it easier for girls and boys to play together and to break free from traditional gender patterns in many (but not all) play practices'. Anggard drew out four major themes from the children's play in a natural environment: war and superhero; family; animal and physical play. The war and superhero play was engaged in only by boys. The family play was mainly girls with the inclusion of a few boys who took on traditional male roles, such as fishing in the games, but the animal and physical play was engaged in by genders together. The animal play was rather like family play, but with, for instance, two dads and lots more excitement. However, during the physical play, age seemed much more important than gender.

She concluded that natural materials are not gender coded in the same way as traditional toys and artefacts are and these therefore lend themselves to non-stereotypical gendered play where the materials can be used by both sexes for any purpose.

Children's photographic research

Lester and Russell (2008: 210) tell us that Newman et al. (2006) did some research with children carrying out a photographic project looking at their own positioning and social status within a playground. They found that much of this was gendered, with dominant boys taking up the central areas with football and girls and the less macho boys on the edges. One effeminate boy used to hide at playtime to avoid bullying.

Research findings

Are any of these researchers surprised by their findings? It seems to us that researchers can always prove that which fits their own cultural view of the world! At the moment we despair. We want to read of a scientist whose research on gender differences has suddenly shaken their world view, or ours, whichever that might be.

Perhaps the most thought provoking view on potential gender differences that we have come across is that of journalist/psychologist Pinker (2008), who wonders why sex differences continue to be so controversial. She suggests that males and females do have different approaches to life and that we should not assume that men and women want similar lives. She asks why the male way should be the standard to which women aspire as this route is forced by patriarchy. She suggests that the female approach is the superior one. Her thoughts were certainly not received well by all. Eliot (2010: 313) states that:

> gender does matter, in education and everything else we do as humans. But if we're going to pay attention to sex differences, we have to do it carefully. After eons of unequal rights and opportunities, no one wants to undo recent progress with distorted stereotypes about either boys or girls. The challenge is to acknowledge and use our understanding of sex differences to help children, without turning this knowledge into self-fulfilling prophecies. We need to be aware of boy-girl differences so we can help children compensate for them early on, allowing every child to flourish in his or her strengths, but always looking for opportunities to stretch them in ways that their peers and the broader culture will not.

Non-gender focused research

Some research is carried out without a specific focus on gender, but the scientists discover information relevant to it. For instance, Mayhew et al. (2004) and Mitchell and Reid-Walsh (2002) in Lester and Russell (2008: 137), found in their studies of children's use of their bedrooms, that, in response to parental fears for safety, whereas boys used to be often found in public spaces and girls in their bedrooms, now boys and girls both use their bedrooms as a private space, for 'cyber play'. This phenomenon was found to be more prevalent in middle class families according to a comparative study carried out by Sutton et al. (2007) because children from working class families more often share bedrooms and their families have less money for technology. It would seem to us that this modern 'similarity' found between the behaviours of boys and girls, is possibly one of a worrying kind. As people interested in children's free play and autonomy, we would rather that the findings showed girls now joining in the more frequent use of public space, rather than boys now using their bedrooms more.

We wonder whether research that 'inadvertently' comes across similarities or differences between the sexes may be more objective than that which is carried out specifically to confirm or deny an existing gender schema.

Lester and Russell (2008: 210) say that in her comparative study of children maintaining their identity status in early childhood settings, Brooker (2006) realized that observation alone is not enough for researchers to understand children's actual experiences and understandings. It involves interpretation of that which is seen by adults. Ali has a good example of this. She says:

> I was watching a three-year-old boy playing with Thomas the Tank engines and he called Percy a 'she'. I asked, 'Is Percy a girl then?' and he looked at me scornfully and said, 'No, she's a train!'

The ethics of research with children

Research involving children has some of the same, but some different issues to research involving adults. Techniques used to find out how children understand things, such as their gender identity, is part of the ongoing debate. What are the issues?

In her paper on the ethics of social research with children and young people, Morrow (n.d.: 12) suggests that 'an over-reliance on one type of data collection method can lead to biases' and further suggests that 'drawing on a range of creative methods and using multiple research strategies' is the way forward. For example, 'The Mosaic Approach' developed in the context of research and taking account of the following: children as social actors in the research process (Mayall 2002); Participatory Appraisal techniques (Hart 1997) which give a voice to the least powerful in society and the Reggio Emilia approach which values the child as competent, strong, capable and resilient. How do these notions work juxtaposed with those that favour the idea that adults can better analyse the thoughts, feelings and actions of children, than children themselves? If we consider that as Jordan-Young (2011: 249) suggests, '[g]ender is a particularly powerful cognitive schema' and particularly take into consideration Holland's conclusions (2003/08: 96) that, '[t]here is no absolute known truth about how children develop and learn and the body of knowledge and understanding grows and changes constantly', they illustrate how children adopt their gender identities. A large body of research has documented that attributions of gender profoundly shape the way observers perceive emotions and behaviour in children and this must include how they act out their gender scripts.

It is particularly pertinent that recent research has shown that the plasticity of the brain and its ability to develop and change is not merely a childhood thing but continues throughout our lives. We find it strange to think that we adults no more own our own behaviour than children do. We are indeed a bundle of ever-changing cells that respond to our internal chemistry and external stimuli without us seemingly being able to do anything about it. Unless, of course, we become super aware of what is going on and try to exert some intelligent effort to enable us to escape the inevitable effects on our own thought processes, of the body we have and the life we lead. Even then, our abilities and perception are not necessarily under our own control. The more science finds out about things, the more we realize that we know less than we think we do. The need for reflective practice becomes even more acute!

Do we, therefore, believe that children's own thoughts, feelings and actions about gender are less valid than adults? McGuffey in conversation with Kane (2013: 113), says: 'Children's agency and adult influences continually recreate produce and change the meanings of gender and sexuality throughout childhood [...] research has shown that peer groups, rather than parents, are often a better predictor of children's behaviour and long-term outcomes.' Holland (2003/08: 22) thinks that sex identity is significant in a child's development of self-image and, therefore, states: 'It is not unreasonable to conjecture that a child would be selecting gender-related characteristics in this construction of ideal self.' This would suggest that both children and adults views on gender are equally valid. If we hark back to our own childhoods and the thoughts and feelings that we had then, we believe that they had just as much validity as those that we think and feel now, only then they were not contaminated with so much life, so much knowledge, so much development, so much a sense of superiority over children.

Children are seen as being disadvantaged by age, social status and powerlessness and protecting children from harm and exploitation is often carried by adults, beyond the ethical necessity for them to ensure that children are not taken advantage of, to seeing all children as a homogenous group who are vulnerable and incompetent. It is important to respect children's competencies and to understand that they are not victims of life, but social actors within it. Therefore, they are just as able to affect their own gender identities as adults are. Further it is important to acknowledge as understood by UNICEF (2010: 10) that gendered experiences are also varied between groups of girls and boys. No group is entirely homogenous – 'all include members of social sub-groups, defined by age, religion, race, ethnicity, economic status, caste, citizenship, sexual identity, ability/ disability, and urban/rural locality'. The experience of a child in one culture may be very different to that of a child in another, even where there are perceived similarities in some gendered behaviour.

Conclusions

Where does this leave us now? We see that there are examples that show that boys and girls play in the same way or that they play differently. We find that in some circumstances they will play in the same way but that play behaviours are generally observed to be the largest form of difference between boys and girls. We discover that there are many and varied forms of research, undertaken by a wide range of scientists from a wide-range of disciplines that spawn conclusions about how sex and gender are 'formed' or 'performed' and there are just as many conclusions about the supposed differences and similarities between the male and female of our species that are the result of this. There are also numerous reasons given as to why it might be important to consider the issues related to differences between the sexes, connected with equality, health and wellbeing, educational support, play needs, marketing and the media and so on.

We said we would return to our 'Category D' which consists of people who believe that there may (or may not) be differences between males and females/boys and girls, but rather than bothering about this, they are concerned with the issues that affect children in the here and now. The issues of concern related to gender and sex for us who work with children at play now, are mainly twofold. Firstly they are related to equality of opportunity for the right for girls and boys to play freely and to express themselves through play, in the here and now and also in relation to their futures if you believe that expressions of gender and sexuality through play have a bearing on this.

Secondly, we have to balance our duty of care to protect children from harm against their need to explore and experiment and to express every aspect of themselves through play, including their gender and sexuality. Are we offering an environment and ambience that fulfils their individual and group play needs and that is not adulterated by adult intervention into this? Do we believe that the way that children play out their gender and sex scripts, during childhood, affects them throughout their developing life cycle and if so how can we balance support for freely chosen play against our concerns for their future? We purport that play is not so much about the future, but more about the present. However, this is not everyone's view and some people may wish that the 'now' is not as it is. How effective can those of us who work with children at play, be against what is considered the genderscape of life and the sexualization of childhood?

All the research findings that we have examined claim to have answers and to come from an un-biased perspective, but we are still not sure that this is demonstrated. In our minds there are no conclusions, there are only more questions to be reflected upon. As Holland (2003/08: 9–10) says:

> In order to be reflective practitioners and to develop practice which has sound foundations, I believe we must be prepared to examine our own stories and to interrogate those most deeply held moral convictions which can make us deaf to the needs and understandings of children

And we believe the same.

Suggested Reading

Anggard, E. (2011), 'Children's Gendered and Non-Gendered Play in Natural Spaces' *Children, Youth and Environments* 21 (2): 5–33. Available online: http://www.colorado.edu/journals/cye (accessed 12 August 2014).

Brown, C. S. (2014), *Parenting Beyond Pink and Blue: How To Raise Your Kids Free of Gender Stereotypes*, New York: Ten Speed Press.

Jordan-Young, R. (2011), *Brainstorm – The Flaws in the Science of Sex Difference*, Cambridge, MA: Harvard University Press.

Lippa, R. A. (2005), *Gender, Nature and Nurture*, New York: Psychology Press.

Pfaff, D. W. (2011), *Man and Woman – An Inside Story*, Oxford: Oxford University Press.

Shibley-Hyde, J. (2005), 'The Gender Similarities Hypothesis', *American Psychologist*. Available online: http://www.areerpioneernetwork.org/wwwrook/user (accessed 9 April 2014).

CHAPTER FIVE

Implications for boys and girls playing – children, sex and sexuality

Introduction

We have decided to devote a chapter exclusively to the subject of children and sexuality and how this is manifested in their playing, in order to:

- clarify terms;

- introduce some of our own research; and

- address the variety of perspectives and reactions that this generates.

Children and sexuality remains a contentious topic in Western society and continues to provoke a range of responses that are often highly subjective, as other authors over the years have also found (see Jackson [1982], Jenkins [1998], Levine [2002], Luker [2007]). Do read this chapter with an open mind and be aware of your own intellectual and emotional responses as you think over the questions and issues we raise!

How we view children's sexuality – indeed, whether we even consider them as sexual beings – is very much a reflection of our own family and cultural heritage and the times in which we live. As is often the case, we can assume that our views are objective and normal until we recognize that not only has our own society shifted in terms of its practices and attitudes (even in the quite recent past), but that other societies may also see things differently, both currently and historically. To begin to address the complexities involved in perceptions of children and sexuality, we seriously need to raise our own awareness about the range of opinions, beliefs and behaviours which, across years and continents, shape and reshape the worlds in which children themselves then have to come to terms with their bodies and sexual identities. This will involve exploring the work of historians, scientists, sociologists, psychologists, psychiatrists and anthropologists, as well as listening to parents and teachers and others who have worked or do work with children.

We begin by asking whether a prepubescent child has a sexuality. This is a difficult topic to discuss rationally not just in the light of current concerns about paedophilia and child sexual exploitation (CSE), but also because sexuality has a number of contexts and may mean different things to different people and we will need to reinterpret this query by asking further practical questions to get us thinking. We will go on to explore the issues that they raise and then return to them at the end of the chapter, but for now, ask yourself what answers you would give to the following – remembering these are about children before they reach puberty.

Key questions

- Are children able to experience sexual pleasure?

- Do (all) children masturbate and, if so, from what age?

- Can children experience orgasm?

- If children can physically experience sexual pleasure, do they need sexual knowledge in order to understand or make sense of their experience?

- Does having such knowledge – at any age – help or hinder their understanding?

- If a child does not have sexual knowledge, does that mean that any physical pleasure they may experience is non-sexual?

- If children behave in apparently sexual ways, are they motivated by the same needs and wants as adults?

- Are there 'milestones' of sexual development that children pass through? And are these the same for all children?

- Can children be 'corrupted'?

- Should children remain innocent of sexual matters for as long as possible? And would that be their preference?

- Are children who experience any form of sexual abuse automatically traumatized?

- Do/can children know their sexual preferences in terms of gender?

- Do children engage in sexual play? And, if so, do all children do this? Is it 'normal'?

- Is sexual play healthy or can it be harmful?

● How can we tell the difference between sexual play, sexual experience and sexual abuse?

Historical/cultural context

Very little research on childhood sexuality has been undertaken, which perhaps is ethically understandable in the present day – most research in the last few decades has focused on childhood sexual abuse. For the few who have undertaken research into 'normative' childhood sexuality and published their findings, the response in the West, in some cases has been extremely negative and some have even attempted to damage the reputations of the researchers (see Rind et al. [1998], Levine [2002]). In our case, too, when we undertook workshops exploring some of the questions raised in the preceding section, we, certainly, received our own share of highly charged complaints (interestingly, always from people who had heard about the workshops, but did not attend them).

As Bancroft (2003: xii) says, 'rational debate and scientific inquiry into *normal* childhood sexual development are currently very difficult' (the italics are ours). Why is this? Jenkins (1998), a historian, describes 'cycles of moral panic' about child sexual abuse that have recurred three times over the last 120 years that significantly affect the way we perceive children and sexuality. We are currently in one of these cycles in the West and so any manifestations of sexualized behaviour by children tend to ring our safeguarding alarm bells. Renold (2005: 21), however, laments that, 'such is the denial of children's sexual awareness, that any child's early interest in sex can be interpreted as warning sign that the child has been sexually abused'. Reynolds et al. (2003: 134) also caution that:

> without a more complete picture of normal childhood sexual behaviours and development, not only will parents and teachers be at a disadvantage with dealing with 'normal' children, interpretation of the abuse literature will be hazardous.

This is somewhat worrying – indeed in our own research, we have heard first-hand many stories of children being referred to Social Services and/or child psychologists and, in some cases, even being put on a sexual offenders' register for what – when viewed through a different lens – appears to be behaviour that is simply a manifestation of curiosity – playing mums and dads at five-years old in the den, for example, or an eleven-year-old boy trying to catch and kiss shrieking girls.

How did we get to this point? There are many converging factors – historical, social, cultural, familial, economic and political – that others, including Jenkins (1998) and Levine (2002), have explored in more detail than we propose to here. Put simply, since the 1980s, there has been growing public concern about child abuse and child sexual abuse, in particular. Parental fears about strangers and paedophiles are widespread and have been fanned by the media (despite the facts that child abduction rates have not risen for sixty years and that the majority of child abuse is from people known to and trusted by the child). Child protection services have been constantly reorganizing and reviewing practice in order to better detect and support children who may have been sexually abused. Books for and by survivors have flooded bookshop shelves and helplines are regularly advertised on our televisions. Definitions of what constitutes abuse have also been revised and updated and new laws have been introduced in order to further protect children. All of this cannot help but influence current societal thinking.

Looking further back in history, we also need to understand that our view of childhood itself has changed regularly over the last few centuries in terms of what we believe their needs and capabilities to be. 'Childhood itself is a historically and culturally fluid social construction; a dynamic product of social processes that changes in concert with social forces and activist efforts' (Kane 2013: 5). There have been times – not so long ago – when children were considered able to work from a young age to help support their families, children were deemed able to reproduce once they had entered puberty, children were not kept from all kinds of 'adult' knowledge, children were also seen as quite willing and capable of seduction. A legal age of consent – the age at which it was considered a child could competently consent to sexual acts – didn't become widely acceptable in the West until the eighteenth century and it has slowly risen ever since as the focus on child exploitation and welfare has increased.

With this backdrop, it is hard to discuss the sexuality of children without reaction and misunderstanding, but we feel it is essential that we do. We need to put aside the Victorian prudishness that still pervades our public psyche, question our assurance that we always know what is best for children and examine our swift objections to alternative perspectives. Our concerns about our children's innocence and protection are not necessarily replicated across the world in other societies, who perceive children as more able and/or having the right to know about sex and sexuality. Jackson (1982: 56) observes that:

> in other cultures who have a more positive and less secretive attitude to sexuality, children have no difficulty in assimilating the sexual information at their disposal. They learn early that sex is pleasurable, incorporate it unselfconsciously into their games and as they mature, gradually replace play by more adult forms of sexual expression.

Concerns about the effects of sexual abuse are also dissimilar elsewhere – Montgomery's (2010) research into child prostitution in Thailand describes a concern there with the children's physical welfare, but no such belief that they are irreparably psychologically damaged and the children in the study did not consider themselves as victims, but rather felt able to positively contribute to the family income. Jackson (1982: 62) postulates that in Western culture 'most of the 'trauma' is probably caused by 'adult reaction', a thought also echoed by Meyer-Bahlburg (2003: 373) when she describes seeing 'marked exacerbation of the effects of child sexual abuse by what happens as a consequence of agency interventions'.

Let us clarify – we are not saying that sexual abuse of children is of no real consequence. We believe it is deplorable – as is all other abuse of children – but that it is so, due to the imbalance of power it comprises. After a great deal of reading, listening and questioning, we also believe that children are not asexual and that our strong desire to keep them safe and 'innocent' often erodes their own defences, undermines their growing confidence, denies them knowledge and understanding and fails to recognize their own experiences and queries. To explain this perspective, we will need to explore further a number of threads and ask you to bear with us as we do so.

Sexual play

We will do this by starting where we began – with children's play. Years ago, we were at a conference and a speaker – an anthropologist – had been talking about children's dens and forts in play spaces and the importance of privacy in childhood. It sparked a discussion and one playworker began to talk about den building being banned on certain local authority play sites because of the concern and/or possibility of children sexually abusing other children. Some playworkers were vociferous about how this practice was violating children's rights to play and to privacy, with one or two cautiously raising the issue of children's growing sexual awareness and how this surely manifested itself in their playing. A number of us at the time continued the discussion and bemoaned the fact that the problem was that none of us knew exactly what was 'normal' because it simply wasn't talked about. As Pellegrini (2009: 97) comments, 'sexual play has been widely discussed in nonhuman play literature [...] but descriptions of sex play among children are very scarce indeed'.

This resonated deeply with us – Ali particularly had been specializing in training playworkers, youth workers and foster carers on childhood sexual abuse and focusing on the child's perspective. Like Egan and Hawkes (2008: 365), we felt that 'the rights of children as sexual subjects are often singularly framed as the right of protection from sexual exploitation, but rarely do these conversations turn toward the equally important right of sexual agency'. How do children 'normally' express this agency? We decided to make an attempt to find out.

Several years later, after trawling the literature and gathering stories and anecdotes, we realize that we cannot use the word 'normal' as this would indicate experiences common to all children and while there are some common experiences and behaviours, these do not extend to all children, do not necessarily occur at certain ages and are described and felt very differently in individuals' stories. We do use the word 'normative' however, to describe experiences that typically occur, but still use this with caution as every child is different and many still may not experience what is labelled 'normative'.

In order to find out what others in our profession thought, we teamed up with a male colleague who was an experienced playworker and who had also in the past been involved in sex education. Together we designed a day's workshop, to be delivered to people who work with children at play, that raised concerns, issues and questions and encouraged them to think, to discuss and to bring forward (either verbally or in writing and anonymously if they wished) their own stories and anecdotes – of their own personal childhood experiences and/or of current incidents and happenings in their workplaces. The workshop was entitled 'One of the Last Taboos' and those who chose to attend knew that it was exploring childhood sexuality and sexual play in particular. We ran the workshop over a dozen times in different parts of the UK and between twelve and twenty people attended each one – in some cases we ran it over two days to maximize time for reflection and discussion. We are very grateful to all the participants for their honesty, their willingness to often face their fears and discomfort and for the stories and scenarios they gave us.

This was an attempt to gather views and information rather than be a carefully crafted piece of scientific research and we also were conscious of the need for sensitivity to different people with diverse experiences and feelings. Nevertheless, it produced some interesting results, provoked fascinating debate and gave the opportunity to air concerns about everyday practice, as many workers were regularly facing children's blunt questions (an eight-year-old asking 'what's a blowjob?', for example) or seeing sexualized behaviours and games or having to deal with potentially abusive incidents and they were uncertain about some of their responses and decisions.

Children, of course, are rarely away from adult eyes these days and so sexual play and testing out the use of sexual language and exploring sexual knowledge that in the past usually occurred alone or between children in privacy – is now more likely to be noticed and/or heard than it used to be. Playworkers, in particular, are often in a unique position to observe and hear this, because they create and oversee 'compensatory play spaces' as children have far less freedom to play than in previous generations and thus children in play settings benefit from the permissional approach of playworkers which enables them to 'determine and control the content and intent of their play, by following their own instincts, ideas and interests, in their own way for their own reasons' (see Playwork Principles [2005], referenced Appendix A).

This meant that we could gather information and stories about children's current activities and experiences without directly setting out to discover this – 'asking children directly about their sexual experience and behaviours is fraught with methodological problems' (O'Sullivan 2003: 27) let alone the ethical considerations of doing so. Together with the retrospective recollections of those workshop participants who were willing to share them (although we do recognize that these can also 'be subject to biases in recall and [...] faulty memory' (2003: 28) we also felt that at present these are 'the most reasonable methods for studying childhood sexual experiences, particularly those that occur during the development phase when secrecy prevails' (Reynolds et al., 2003: 135) and all these anecdotes do give a broad picture of diverse childhood sex play encounters – past and present – across the age range.

One exercise in our workshop was to list some sexual behaviours and ask participants to decide in each case when they thought these might first manifest themselves in children and young people's lives.

Reflective questions

What might you answer? At what age do you think these might first occur in/between children?

- Kissing and cuddling
- Masturbation
- You show me yours, I'll show you mine
- Touching other's private parts (same gender)
- Touching other's private parts (opposite gender)
- Orgasm
- Oral sex
- Intercourse

Phrasing the question this way makes it a cognitive exercise but in reality our answers are likely to reflect our own experiences (of ourselves and of others), as we have no other real way of 'knowing'.

The range of answers we collected were as follows

Kissing and cuddling	0–1 yrs
Masturbation	0–1 yrs
You show me yours, I'll show you mine	2–4 yrs
Touching other's private parts (same gender)	4–6 yrs
Touching other's private parts (opposite gender)	4–6 yrs
Orgasm	6–12 yrs
Oral sex	7–14 yrs
Intercourse	11–16 yrs

This is quite a wide range of answers and some are considerably younger than many might expect, although apart from intercourse, these were accompanied by playful stories that indicated curiosity and unexpected pleasure often with little understanding that this was 'sexual' – a few examples are given below.

Workshop stories

- A woman described how, as a seven-year-old girl, she repeatedly experienced 'the most amazing beautiful feeling when climbing a rope in the school gym'. She realized in hindsight this would have been orgasm but had no idea at the time – 'I just knew it felt nice and although I remember asking another girl if she felt the same (she didn't) I also instinctively felt I shouldn't talk about it – it was private'.

- A man describing how he mostly played with girls (there were few boys where he lived) and he vividly remembers a recurring and exciting game when he was nine-years-old where they would pretend to be asleep and one of them would try to take the other's clothes off one by one without 'waking' them up. Very occasionally they got completely naked but then they would laugh and get dressed again.

- A woman describing the performance of loving rituals between Sindy and Action Man dolls under her bedclothes at night 'when I was supposed to be reading before turning the light off'. She recalls 'the frisson of hiding the dolls down the bed and getting them to kiss and the anxiety of being caught'. She supposes she was eight- or nine-years old.

- A man describing when in the infant class at primary school, the girl he sat by offered to show him her 'bottom' and pulled her skirt and pants down so he could quickly see. He remembers being fascinated because he only had brothers and had never seen a girl before.

- A woman describing how a boy on her table at school got his willy out under the table and tried to get everyone else to do the same – 'we were six because I remember the teacher'. She remembers looking with interest but then they were discovered and were all sent home. She remembers being lectured by the headmaster and 'made to feel appalling and dirty' and told never ever to do this again. She recalls feeling terribly ashamed but also confused because she had only looked and didn't understand why this was so wrong.

- A man describing how he (aged seven) and another boy in his class had been playing in his bathroom and had taken their shorts and pants off and danced around the room laughing. He remembers feeling flushed and excited and having an erection and then playing boats in the basin.

- A woman describing how at aged ten, she and another boy in her class would regularly go to the gully on the way home from school and practise 'French kissing – it was really nice'.

- A man describing how on holiday each year he would meet and play with the same girl as they were growing up and each summer they got 'more daring' – moving from showing each other their bodies at aged six or seven through to kissing and touching at aged eight and kissing each other's genitals at aged nine or ten. 'It was really mutual and felt very natural.' This all happened sporadically in the woods behind their campsite in between all kinds of other 'non-sexual' games.

- A woman describing how her brother (he was fourteen and she was ten) came into her bedroom and asked her if he could try something out on her and promised her chocolate if she would. 'I can't remember what he tried to do although looking back I suspect he was attempting intercourse but he certainly didn't succeed. Years later I briefly berated myself on behaving like a prostitute, but actually – having no knowledge of prostitutes when I was ten, I felt fine with it at the time and enjoyed the chocolate!'

These stories also concur with Friedrich's (2003: 119) findings when he conducted studies of the sexuality of non-abused children and concluded that 'sexual behaviour in children is typically non-pathologic, follows a developmental course and can be quite varied'. A few others have researched forms of sex play – notably Thorne and Luria (1986), Lamb and Coakley (1993), Reynolds and Herbenick (2003), Sandfort and Rademakers (2000). Some have asked caregivers to complete observations of their young children against a Child Sexual Behaviour Inventory (CSBI) and others have asked adults to reminisce and recall experiences when they were children.

Poole and Wolfe (2009: 109) in their exploration of normative sexual behaviour in childhood, say that 'adults who remember and recount childhood experiences report a considerable amount of undiscovered sexual behaviour' and refer to retrospective studies that featured examples of children exhibiting their bodies, masturbation and genital fondling, oral sex and attempted intercourse in middle childhood (6–12 years).

All these studies and our own collected stories, do propose that sexual play is a common phenomenon among many children, primarily motivated by curiosity and they challenge recent prevailing views that: a) children are asexual in their thinking and their behaviour; and b) that children in middle childhood do not – and should not – engage in sexual behaviour. Many of the stories we heard also included tellings off and punishments meted out by adults who discovered or overheard them and the guilt or confusion that followed.

Such prevailing views do tend to drive children's experiences underground – they learn quite early on that most adults are embarrassed by their questions and disapprove of them behaving in certain ways. It does seem to be the case that the 'abuse rhetoric has also expanded medicalized and deviant labels over juvenile sexual behaviours that until very recently were commonly regarded as harmless play' (Jenkins 2003: 13).

Jackson takes the view that children are not asexual but neither are they fully sexual beings as they also lack awareness and understanding of their experiences. Encounters and events in childhood take on new meaning and 'become' sexual through later reinterpretation when they know more of the facts. Jackson (1982: 80) calls this 'protosexual learning' – 'isolated or arbitrary incidents that may, when placed in the context of sexual knowledge later on, have some sexual significance'.

Reflective questions

How much sexual knowledge should children have? Is too little – or too much – harmful? How relevant is their age?

Sex Education

Levine (2002: 8) suggests that 'our crudest and oldest fear about letting out too much sexual information is that it will lead kids to try this at home as soon as they are able'. O'Sullivan (2003: 24) however states 'there is substantial evidence that educating children about sexuality matters does not produce adverse consequences such as prompting early onset of sexual behaviour'. It seems that censorship is not the same as protection.

Or is it that we are worried about 'disturbing' children or upsetting them if we say too much too early? We may remember feeling disturbed or even revolted ourselves when we discovered the basic facts about sexual activity – especially when we realized our parents must have also done this! Jackson (1982: 106) thinks that this is because information comes all at once culminating in a sudden shocking realization, whereas 'learning gradually means children can accept sexual knowledge without difficulty'.

Many parents do have 'the conversation' on one occasion when they feel it has become necessary and often find it embarrassing; many others still say little or nothing to their children about sex, preferring to leave them to discover the facts for themselves or from their school teachers. And what is the content of 'the conversation' or of school sex education lessons? This does vary from country to country, but certainly in many western societies, it mostly seems to be about the 'birds and the bees', the biological facts about reproduction which is the consequence of sex – and very little about sex itself. Jackson (1982: 148) puts it well when she asks 'we hardly need precise knowledge of the digestive system in order to organize our diet effectively, so why is it thought so important to understand fertilization, implantation and foetal development before we manage our sexuality?'

Sex education tends to be sanitized, moralistic and concentrates on the future, so that children get to know about babies but know very little about sexuality, about desire and arousal, about foreplay and pleasure, about making love, about homosexuality and about how any of this relates to them in the present. Girls particularly can therefore go years before ever finding out about their clitoris and its real function. Children, therefore, discover most sexual information from each other – which could include myths and falsehoods – and/or from the internet, which is likely to include pornography that is usually full of macho scripts and often comprizes violence. Goedele Liekens, a UN ambassador for sexual health and campaigner for a school-based curriculum that teaches children about sexual pleasure and consent, believes that if we 'shy away from discussing sex in explicit detail, we lose all chance of counteracting porn's disastrous effect on our young people' (2015). There are a few websites that are set up for children and young people that are really positive and informative and include the facility to have questions – however explicit – answered, but we have not come across any adults or children's organizations yet who promote them.

Children and young people are streets ahead of adults in terms of technology and whether we like it or not and whether we try and prevent it or not, they will be accessing sites and images that we know little about and probably don't care for. Would it not be better to open up genuine conversation about what they are seeing and trying to make sense of? There is also some recent research (Voon et al. 2014) that may indicate that regular watching of pornography can affect the brain in possibly two ways: a) to change arousal centres so that watching becomes necessary for arousal rather than participating in real life; and b) that certain reward centres in the brain associated with addiction are activated, driving the viewer to watch more and more. If this is true, we do find that worrying.

Gagnon and Simon (1973) postulated that we learn about sexuality and eventually act out sexual roles from socially learned scripts, rather than acting on biologically driven sexual impulses, and they draw our attention to consider what those scripts might be and indeed which scripts we may have learnt. Have we wrestled with guilt, anxiety and confusion about our own sexuality and sexual behaviour, derived from the secrecy that surrounded it during our formative years? If we disapprove of children's sexual curiosity and find it difficult to answer their questions, what message does that give them? If children learn about sexual acts from watching pornography, with no opportunity to talk about what they see, will they be espousing biased and macho scripts? How are they affected by the sexualization that Bailey (2011) calls 'the wallpaper of children's lives'– in terms of fashion, language, popular culture, music – products that are marketed to children that we all might label sexy or sexual? Is it okay for preschool girls to wear thongs, dance provocatively and sing lyrics like 'baby, I'm so hot for you'? Is it okay for little boys to wear T-shirts emblazoned 'chick magnet', dance aggressively while muttering 'I'll get you motherfucker'? Have they any idea what the words mean? Are they learning anything from all this? Are Levin and Kilbourne (2008: 5) right to say that 'children are paying an enormous price for the sexualization of their childhood? Girls and boys constantly encounter sexual messages and images that they cannot understand and that can confuse and even frighten them'? Rush and La Nauze (2006) even describe advertising and marketing which sexualizes children as 'corporate paedophilia'.

On the other hand, the research of Buckingham et al. (2010) on sexualized goods aimed at children seems to indicate that children are not passive recipients but skilled consumers, reinterpreting purchases with different meanings according to children's culture – the Playboy bunny image, for instance, became for them a symbol of a good student. If children do not know what something means, how can it influence them in the ways adults assume? As Levin and Kilbourne (2008: 21) admit, we tend to use an adult lens for interpreting what children say about sex, rather than a child's lens, and 'often when adults think "sex", children have something very different on their minds'.

Over and over in the discussions where adults voice their concerns about children and sex; what children do and don't know, what they should and shouldn't know, how they do and don't behave and how they should or shouldn't behave – there is an underlying powerful thread of adult responsibility that rarely acknowledges children's own agency and ability to make sense of things, or attempts to see children's responses to all things sexual through their eyes. It does seem that we adults career on with our debates and arguments on morals and on values and don't take sufficient time to sit outside ourselves and listen to and evaluate what is really going on in ourselves, our children and our society – and other societies who deal with all this rather differently.

Jackson (1982: 160) wrote the following over thirty years ago and we're not sure that in Western society we've made much progress since.

> None of the difficulties surrounding sex education would exist if we did not treat children as a special category of people and sexuality as a special area of life. The best that schools – a product of the former practice – can do is to try to challenge the latter. The way to do this is not through formal, separate sex education programmes, but through discussing sexual matters wherever they are relevant, in all areas of the curriculum and throughout children's school careers. The problem, once again, is not how to tell children about sex, but how to stop concealing it from them.

This sentiment of course equally applies to parents and to other professionals who work with children – shouldn't we all be able to talk with children and answer their questions without fear of reprisal and without fear of upsetting or corrupting them? But might there be more to our fear and concern over children and sex than we have so far explored in this chapter? Perhaps if 'the social recognition of children as sexual citizens is still ideologically tethered to what adults deem to be socially acceptable sexuality' (Egan and Hawkes 2008: 365), then as Luker (2007: 201) suggests our worries may be actually more deeply embedded in our beliefs about gender – and heterosexuality in particular.

Heteronormativity

Gender and sexuality seem to be inextricably linked when we regard the messages given to young children including those through books and media. Little boys and little girls are 'expected' to one day fall in love and partner someone of the opposite gender. While there are a few children's books now in circulation about homosexuality and having either two daddies or two mummies, these are not on every home or nursery's bookshelf and if we are honest our own expectation that young children will turn out to be heterosexual rolls off the tongue. This may be unwitting because until recently that has been the 'norm' or it may be rooted in conscious homophobia to a greater or lesser degree. Time and again, we hear those who work with children telling us how fathers in particular insist that their sons do not dress up while in their care and many have witnessed boys being told off for doing so – 'I won't have you behaving like a puff'.

This 'enforced heterosexuality' has been termed 'heteronormativity' (see Chapter 2) by social scientists and those researching its' manifestation in children's lives illustrate that it has quite an effect. We regularly see girls play at weddings and fantasize about their future 'husbands' and hear boys teasing each other – sometimes quite nastily – about being gay. Butler (1990) put forward her 'heterosexual matrix' based on the assumptions made in the West about the development of sexuality. Put simply, this 'matrix' purports that anatomical sex ascribed at birth leads to gender identity formation, which then leads to the development of sexual desire for the opposite sex. In other words, a baby with a penis will become a 'masculine' boy who will desire girls and women, and a baby with a vagina will become a 'feminine' girl who will desire boys and men. As Renold states (2005: 8) Butler herself 'exposes (this) developmental path of sex, gender and desire to be wholly illusory and further illustrates [...] how this illusion is maintained through the policing and shaming of 'abnormal' or 'Other sexual/gendered identities'.

If we remember – as we alluded to in the first chapter – that 'gender is a complex, multidimensional concept, not simply a binary of two fixed categories, male and female' (Kane 2013: 19) then our understanding of both gender and sexuality starts to shift. Studying intersexuality, transgendered people and a wide variety of sexual orientations reveals the 'interconnected but distinct categories of gender identity and sexuality and the fluidity of such categories' (2013: 15).

Intersex

It's worth pausing for a moment to consider the slowly growing recognition and range of intersex people. They may be born with ambiguous genitalia (currently between 1 in 1,500 and 1 in 2,000 births). They may appear to be either female or male on the outside but internally have mostly the 'opposite' anatomy. They may have a genetic condition whereby some of their cells have XY chromosomes and others have XX. There are a whole variety of hormonal and chromosomal traits and conditions that fall within the intersex spectrum. Obtaining accurate statistics of the incidence of all these conditions is impossible as records are not routinely kept; many of these conditions do not become apparent until puberty or until trying to conceive and many people wish to remain silent about it.

Estimates for intersex people vary from 0.05 per cent to 4 per cent of the population, although Organisation Intersex International Australia (2013) recommend a midrange figure of 1.7 per cent, supported by Anne Fausto-Sterling, Professor of Biology and Gender Studies at Brown University, Rhode Island. Preves (2005: 2–3) contests that 'physical sexual ambiguity occurs about as often as the well-known conditions of cystic fibrosis or Down's syndrome' and that 'distinctions between male and female bodies are actually on more of a continuum than a dichotomy'. This reality has dogged the sporting world for a long time – the hormonal and/or chromosomal criteria for establishing whether an athlete is male or female keep changing as new participants keep turning up that don't 'fit'. When we consider that almost every aspect of our lives is organized or categorized by our gender (and even more so during childhood), then that might explain the medical profession's haste in performing early surgery in order to assign and attribute a gender to a new baby – we simply cannot envisage how to raise a child that isn't a girl or a boy (isn't it the first question we all ask new parents?) and we make the assumption that it would certainly be traumatic for the child. Sadly, such surgery has often proved to be traumatic in these children's lives – especially if they later feel that their assigned gender is not compatible with the gender identity they have come to feel is theirs.

How often does it cross the minds of us professionals that some of the children we work with might not be a girl or a boy as we know it? There have been times both in history and in other present societies when a 'third' sex is either discretely or warmly recognized. At the time of writing, seven countries have birth registration records that have three 'gender boxes' – Germany was the most recent to introduce them.

Potential Answers

So times are slowly changing, as they always do, and our views on both gender and sexuality have certainly been challenged in the last fifty years (and hopefully in this book!). And, as always, children themselves are also active in their attempts to make sense of the cultural messages they receive, which may involve periods of both passivity and resistance.

If we return to the questions posed at the beginning of this chapter, we are in a position to address these, although there is still much to learn.

- Are children able to experience sexual pleasure?

   Yes it would seem so

- Do (all) children masturbate and if so, from what age?

   If by masturbation, we mean manipulating genital organs, then it seems not all, but many do at different times and can do from babyhood

- Can children experience orgasm?

   If by orgasm we mean an intensely pleasurable bodily feeling that emanates from the genitals, it seems so

- If children can physically experience sexual pleasure, do they need sexual knowledge in order to understand or make sense of their experience?

   They can only understand it as 'sexual pleasure' if they have knowledge of sexual function

- Does having such knowledge – at any age – help or hinder their understanding?

   If that knowledge – at any age – is relevant, meaningful and either imparted or discovered in a way that makes sense to the child, then such knowledge can surely only be helpful

- If a child does not have sexual knowledge does that mean that any physical pleasure they may experience is non-sexual?

   It is probably impossible to answer this as what constitutes 'knowledge' and what is defined as 'sexual' varies hugely and may be experienced differently by individual children

● If children behave in apparently sexual ways, are they motivated by the same needs and wants as adults?

> Pre-pubescent children can experience interest and pleasure, but this is different to post-puberty and again to adulthood as understanding, desire, sexual experience and levels of hormones increase

● Are there 'milestones' of sexual development that children pass through and are these the same for all children?

> Further research is really necessary; there seem to be a few general markers but these don't necessarily apply to all children – the idea of 'milestones' is far too prescriptive and many inter-weaving factors (social, emotional, familial, environmental, cultural, religious, gender) influence the precipitation of explorative 'sexual' behaviour in childhood

● Can children be 'corrupted' by sexual experience or sexual knowledge?

> What is meant by the term 'corruption'? Children who are repeatedly sexually abused are certainly affected by their experiences and may need to relearn more 'normative' behaviour and may require therapeutic support. But giving children information about sex and sexuality is educative, not 'corruptive'

● Should children remain innocent of sexual matters for as long as possible and would that be their preference?

> Our view on this is that we should follow children's lead and answer their questions honestly as they grow up

● Are children who experience any form of sexual abuse automatically traumatized?

> This is questionable. Some children do get upset; some may become distressed; some are traumatized, but not all are – some seem to be unaffected. It is so widely assumed that any child with any abusive experience will be traumatized, that this can become a self-fulfilling prophecy and certainly the reaction from adults has a huge effect. We have heard stories from adults who went to counselling believing they must have blocked something out because they were not suffering from some incident in their past and were worried that they should be

● Do/can children know their sexual preferences in terms of gender?

> Some children do question this at a young age – many gay

adults say in hindsight that they always 'knew' they were not straight

● Do children engage in sexual play and if so do all children do this and is it 'normal'?

   Many (but seemingly not all) children do at different times – as with all other forms of play, it is their way of making sense of their world

● Is sexual play healthy or can it be harmful?

   If all children involved are freely playing of their own volition, it seems to be explorative fun. If they are not freely playing, it may be harmful to a greater or lesser degree (i.e. discomfort ranging to actual abuse) as there may be coercion involved

● Can we tell the difference between sexual play, sexual experience and sexual abuse?

   Perhaps we can – sexual play is mostly pre-pubescent when children are curious and finding out what they don't know. Sexual experience denotes physical involvement (although this could still be playful in content!) with oneself or consensually with peers with at least some knowledge of sexual matters. Sexual abuse involves the exploitation, persuasion or coercion of a child or young person and may be emotionally and/or physically damaging, but not necessarily so. In Chapter 7, we will explore what are natural and healthy behaviours and what are not

We have hardly scratched the surface of the subject of children and sexuality in this chapter and we will return to it again as seen from other perspectives in Chapter 7, but for now we would all do well to pause and think 'how have our cultural beliefs about childhood and sexuality channelled what we perceive as normal, what we define as a problem and what we ignore or deny?' (Frayser 2003: 255).

Suggested reading

Doidge, N. (2014), 'Sex on the Brain – What Brain Plasticity Teaches About Internet Porn' *Hungarian Review* 4: 3044. Available online: http://www. yourbrainonporn.com/sex-brain-what-brain-plasticity-teaches-about-internet-porn-2014-norman-doidge-md (accessed on 2 February 2015).

Jackson, S. (1982), *Childhood Sexuality*, Oxford: Basil Blackwell.

Kane, E. W. (2013), *Rethinking Gender and Sexuality in Childhood*, London: Bloomsbury.

Levin, D. E. and J. Kilbourne (2008), *So Sexy, So Soon*, New York: Ballantine Books.

Levine, J. (2002), *Harmful to Minors – The Perils of Protecting Children from Sex*, New York: Thunder's Mouth Press.

Papadopolous, L. (2010), *Sexualisation of Young People*, Review Report.

Preves, S. (2005), *Intersex and Identity – the Contested Self*, New Jersey: Rutgers University Press.

Renold, E. (2005), *Girls, Boys and Junior Sexualities*, Oxon: RoutledgeFalmer.

CHAPTER SIX

Adult bias and reflective practice

Introduction

This chapter considers whether adults and those who work with children at play are consciously and/or unconsciously biased in the way that they work, by their own gender and sexuality, by their own experiences, philosophy and/or the emphasis given to particular unproven theories related to the acquisition or performance of gender and sexuality. It will outline the ways that a range of adults react and respond to children's genderized and sexualized play behaviours and consider whether these responses take full account of the overall well-being of the children with whom they work and indeed take account of children's agency and children's rights.

In his 1932 novel, *Brave New World*, Aldous Huxley recognized the insidious way in which our views, those views that we believe are unique to us, are formed:

Not so much like drops of water, though water, it is true, can wear holes in the hardest granite; rather, drops of liquid sealing wax, drops that adhere, incrust, incorporate themselves with what they fall on, till finally the rock is all one scarlet blob.

Till at last the child's mind *is* these suggestions, and the sum of suggestions *is* the child's mind; and not the child's mind only. The adult mind too – all his life long. The mind that judges and desires and decides – made of the suggestions.

We should begin by considering our own views on gender – its role in our own lives and in the lives of those around us. We will move on to looking at sex and sexuality towards the end of the chapter, although it should be noted that in reality these areas of life are not discreet.

What do adults believe?

Do we believe that males and females have naturally different attributes – different strengths and weaknesses, different ways of thinking, feeling and expressing themselves? Or do we think that males and females are similar in most ways and that any differences are socially constructed? Regardless of what we believe, do we actually see males and females behaving in different ways and appearing to have different strengths and weaknesses, different ways of thinking, feeling and expressing themselves? If so, do we think it matters? Why does it matter? Who is advantaged and who is disadvantaged? Are there other areas of life that might have the same advantages and disadvantages?

We carried out a small-scale survey, previously mentioned in Chapter 3, on playworkers who worked in adventure playgrounds and after-school clubs. We asked them the following four questions:

1   Do you think that boys and girls play differently?
2   What evidence do you have to support your answer?
3   Do you think it matters?
4   Do workers have a role to play in this, e.g. if children play in gender stereotypical ways should you intervene or encourage the opposite?

The general response was that girls and boys do play differently and that it did not really matter if it was their choice to do so. Intervention was often around children being left out on the basis of gender rather than because of specific stereotypical gendered behaviour. So the majority of workers questioned said that if, for instance a group of girls said that a boy could not join them in a game because he was a boy (or vice versa), they would explain that boys and girls can do anything that they want. However, several of the workers mentioned the importance of role modelling non-stereotypical male/female behaviour in the playwork setting and said that they made sure that male and female workers all cooked, worked with tools, dealt with accidents, did building and maintenance work and so on. Several also told of direct interventions – when for instance a father had tried to prevent his daughter from using tools because 'they are for boys', the playworker had advocated on the girl's behalf and on another site a playworker had actively encouraged bike riding and going on a risky roundabout for a girl whose father felt that 'girls should do only girl things and boys do boy things'. Several workers mentioned peer involvement and that children like to feel part of the group and so will behave in whatever way facilitates that, which usually involves girls in groups and boys in groups. Some of the workers spoke about loose parts being non-gendered and the importance of providing resources and opportunities that allowed children to explore alternatives and foster cross-gender play.

It is very difficult for anybody to live his or her life in a non-gendered way, such is the force of our collective genderized human behaviour. Burke (1996: 3) wrote: 'When the child emerges into the world, every physical movement and spoken word, every toy touched and game imagined, are coloured by the power of gender role expectations.' Gender is a group activity. West and Fenstermaker (2002: 29) suggests: 'Gender is not simply something one is, but rather it is something one does in interaction with others.' The way in which we behave, maintains and reinforces the behaviour of others and that behaviour becomes group behaviour – the 'right' behaviour. The dominant 'right' behaviour of the west is to be male or female and behave in whatever is considered to be the appropriate masculine or feminine way, for that group, and mainly in support of being heterosexual.

In which case, how much are we influenced in our views about children and their gender expression or development by what we consider to be the 'right' way to think based on our general way of life? And how has that general way of life developed? How many of us take the time to consider all the varying views that there are about gender and whether it is either constructed, developed, performed, expressed, maintained or born? How many of us try to see whether there is truth in any of them and what that truth might be?

Jones (2009: 79) thinks that as an arena of research, gender 'is one that is highly politicized and contested' and any attempt to examine our own attitudes towards children and gender requires us to examine all the differing agendas, such as 'feminists position of challenging inequality and more right wing opposition to ideas about equity' that fuel the different research agendas and philosophies. Only then can we see whether our views on children's gender expression, development or acquisition come from our own philosophical beliefs or from observation of and being with children and from reflection on what Holland (2008: 24–5) calls 'the genderscape of children's lives'. If we are unable to examine our own influences thoroughly and how they affect our working practices, we are unlikely to be in a position to consider the children themselves – our view of their gender development and expression will be muddied by our own view, and that in turn will be limited by that which we have considered but also and particularly by our own experiences of being a gendered person. Emily Kane in interview with Jones (2009: 89) says that it is 'important to recognize children as active agents in their own development, but also to recognize the instances in which adults curtail that agency, as the latter are important barriers to that agency.'

Hughes (2011: 176) suggests that a 'controlled authentic approach' to working with children at play, is both facilitative and empowering. It recognizes that the worker, like the child, is an 'amalgamation of factors, some good, some not so good', and thus the adult is able to 'unself-ishly relinquish control and pass it back to the child'. This then allows the child to be as expert on their own gender and its expressions as the worker. Cranny-Francis et al. (2002: 49) suggest that 'The human subject is never in a pure state of nature', but their free will is 'compromized' by social codes, institutional values and so on – this then makes it even more important that we challenge our firmly held beliefs and check to see if they are truly in the child's best interests (should we be able to ascertain what these are!). In relation to children, adults often suffer from 'unquestionable moral arrogance' always believing that they know best! In his article about our modern addiction to criminalizing human behaviour, journalist Simon Jenkins (2014) says of priests and lawyers that they 'might be perfectly open minded, but their professional background could curse them with dogma, prejudgement and false certainty'. We believe this can sometimes be true of professionals in the early years/childcare/playwork sector who despite having undergone their training, may then fail to see what is going on before their eyes and fail to reflect on their own part in children's behaviour.

Martin (2005) gives an example of this in Jones (2009: 100) when she reports from her research that there is general adult anxiety about 'girls and boys thinking of themselves as similar' as this seems to be associated with advocating homosexuality and she notes that there are few institutions that 'offer suggestions on how to raise people to be gay'! Do we as adults make assumptions about the heteronormativity of the children we work with? If we made the assumption that all the children we worked with were homosexual, would that alter the way that we worked? Would more or less children grow up to be gay? Or do we not think that our approach or values make any difference?

Another example, touched on in Chapter 2 and still being practiced, is related to people, mainly women, believing that by taking toy guns and other toys associated with violence, away from boys and replacing them with more 'creative' toys, we would socialize boys away from violence at an early age. To date this has not been proved to be accurate and Holland (2008: 19) also asserts that: 'Children brought up in anti-sexist homes are just as likely to exhibit stereotyped (gendered) behaviour as children brought up with more traditional gender roles and vice versa'.

Ask any parent or childcare worker whether they think that boys should be stopped from any or all forms of play that have a 'violent' potential to them, such as playing with toy guns and swords, play fighting, war, hunting and so on and you will usually find that they will answer with moral certainty either 'yes' or 'no' as if there is proof that whatever their viewpoint and practice, this will ensure that boys will not go on to become violent adults. As far as we can see, there is no proof, either way. However, just to set the record straight, there does appear to be some evidence that very extreme forms of play deprivation or manifestations of overly sadistic play in childhood, may be an indicator of later psychopathic, violent or extreme anti-social behaviour. For example, Brown in Bekoff and Byers (1998: 247), who conducted a study of a student who went on a killing spree, killing seventeen people and injuring a further thirty-one, concluded

FIGURE 6.1 *Girls will be boys*
Permission granted by Peach

that the conditions which led to his violent and tragically deconstructive behaviour included 'physical and emotional abuse and playlessness'. Brown also finds in further studies of groups, such as alcoholic drunk drivers, that the common factor was that none of them had played in a 'normal' way during their childhoods. Brown and Lomax (1969) further found in a study of twenty-five young murderers that there was evidence of play deprivation and major play abnormalities such as sadism and cruelty in their childhood play. In the media, there have been articles that concur, e.g. Johnston (2011) and S. L. Scott (n.d.) suggests that many children who display evidence of unusually cruel forms of play, often being cruelty to animals, later become delinquents, violent criminals or psychopathic killers. However, as most children know, there is a difference between pretend violence in play and real violence.

A child who has an obsession with dinosaurs does not necessarily become a palaeontologist in adulthood anymore than a child who plays with toy guns or swords becomes an aggressive adult.

As we explored in Chapter 1, playing for children is a spontaneous experience and, while it has all kinds of developmental value, that is not necessarily its whole purpose. A growing body of evidence, Lester and Russell (2008), shows that playing stimulates synaptic connections in the brain that support flexible thinking and emotion regulation rather than learning specific skills for the future – play is as much about 'being' and experiencing the here and now as it is about 'becoming'. The more we truly observe play, the more we see children of all ages constructing their own variation on expectations of gendered behaviour – as the following examples illustrate.

FIGURE 6.2 *Make believe aggression*
Permission granted by King

A girl of three, dressed in very 'girly' clothes and playing with one Ken and several Barbies and other very 'girly' small world dolls, turned a game of 'mums and babies' into 'going to the ocean', where the small dolls (who were dressed as mermaids initially) did various death defying leaps from the cliffs (the bed) into the water (the rug). One of the stereotypically glamorously dressed mums rescued the babies and gave them life saving support. Meanwhile, Ken was cooking tea and entertaining some random visitors (various Barbies). Absolutely no attention was given to the clothes, hairstyles etc. of the Barbies it was all about the antics in the ocean and the dramatic rescues.

Three children, a boy of ten, girl of eight and girl of three, are mooching around together. The eight-year old has some nail varnish and glittery bits to pour onto it. She asks if someone will paint her nails and apply the glitter. An adult offers to do so. The three-year-old declares that it is not fair and the ten-year-old boy offers to do her nails. He concentrates hard and with much smudging and wiping he paints the nails of one hand and pours glitter on. He is totally involved. He then declares he has had enough because it is more difficult than he thought and says that someone else will have to finish it. He goes and picks up a ball. He segues between stereotypical female and male play!

All adults who work with children will have their beliefs and every culture, organization, institution, home, peer group and so on will already have in existence, or will develop its own 'genderscape', i.e. an either implied or explicit code that supports particular ways of being and responding in relation to its members' gender. Holland (2008: 24–5) believes that 'the genderscape created in the early years can limit the options for both boys and girls'. This is certainly true in popular culture with toys and books and clothes – a number of cases have recently been in the news where girls have complained that they cannot buy certain items such as superhero sweat-shirts as they are advertised and marketed only to boys. In reality it requires a great deal of thought as to how these limitations can be countered without the involvement of adult 'unquestionable moral arrogance'!

Reflective question

Do you believe that the 'genderscape' of a child's early years can limit options for boys and girls and if so, in what way?

From their research into differences in gender across different cultures, Aydt and Corsaro (2003) suggest that gender roles are communicated in very subtle ways by adults and because children seek to be valued, they conform to those attributes that are valued by the adults in their own community. Thus, they suggest that we can infer that levels of segregation between boys and girls, in any community, will vary according to the degree that males are considered to be aggressive and females passive. Aydt and Corsaro (2003: 1309) also notice that this causes peer cultures to be different among children of different cultures yet they remark that 'gendered behaviour among children is spoken of monolithically' as if it was the same in all communities. Children's peer genderscapes are not one thing, but many and we believe that unconscious gender stereotyping is alive and kicking.

Gender is a minefield and not least when you are working with children. Parents have responsibility for their children and thus any work with children has to involve consideration of the views and reactions of their parents, who have their own genderized perspectives, but also carry concern about the judgement of others regarding their parenting (we will see this below in an outline of styles of parenting related to gender) and this can make a difference to the way that workers are able to respond to children's gendered behaviour. A girl playing cops and robbers is fine, for example, but a boy playing at being a beautician is often considered, particularly by fathers, not fine. Parents worry about their children being able to 'fit in' and not be considered odd by other children or other adults and so will monitor the levels of gendered conformity they believe are acceptable. While this can and does happen for both boys and girls in different ways, it is sometimes harder for gentle or sensitive boys who can end up being labelled as 'cissy' – something many parents fear. Parents of possibly transgendered children have even greater angst – reading about how both parents and their 'gender-fluid' children navigate daily life is both fascinating and heartbreaking – see the link to such an article in the references for this chapter. But all parents regularly make genderized decisions – with or without thinking first.

Mum was expecting a new baby and so that her little boy, who was three, would not feel left out, she decided to buy him a baby doll that he could feed, bath, dress, cuddle and push around in a toy pushchair. His dad was not keen, but was finally prepared to accept his son having a doll and pushchair as long as it was a baby boy doll dressed in blue, not a baby girl doll dressed in pink that he would be playing with.

Responses to gendered behaviour

We have both worked in the playwork field for many years and based on our experience of having observed or participated in a range of different types of provision for children's play – after-school clubs, adventure playgrounds, playschemes, holiday clubs, specialist children's clubs, school playtimes, crèches, playgroups and so on, we have previously suggested (2012) that there are a number of ways in which we have seen adults respond to the notion of gender at play as outlined below:

Types of responses to gendered play

Gender ignorant

Workers here haven't thought about anything to do with gender at all. So, the play environment is very much based on the personality and experiences of the workers themselves who basically make the assumption that what has worked for them personally (in their own childhoods or previous practice) will be fine for the children they work with now. This practice generally seems to support gender norms.

Gender neutral

Workers here believe that fundamentally there's no difference between boys and girls playing apart from that which has been socially constructed through their prior experiences. Thus, workers create and resource an environment that tries to be non-gendered and believe and expect that given the opportunity, both girls and boys will be happy to have a go at anything and we should just leave them to get on with it. These workers try to be gender blind – they refuse to accept any differences.

Gender controlled

Workers here decide that boys and girls are reluctant to play at that which is considered to be the other gender's forte and so they set out to ensure that stereotypical play will not happen if they can help it. They ban weapons. They encourage girls to play football, pool and rough and tumble. They encourage boys to do creative stuff and dressing up. They intervene in conversations where girls or boys – usually and especially boys – are putting each other down on account of gender. These workers really dislike any displays of stereotypically gendered play and believe that by intervening they can change the status quo and influence children's development.

Gender stereotyped

Workers here decide that girls will be girls and boys will be boys so set out to cater for both by having girly things and macho things and having the male worker outside doing physical stuff and sports and the female worker inside doing creative stuff and cooking. These workers believe that there are natural differences between the play preferences of boys and girls and cater for them accordingly.

Gender similar

Workers here decide to create and resource an environment that will focus on the similarities of boys/girls play. They may, therefore, deliberately encourage games like rounders rather than football on the grounds that both genders like rounders and will happily participate. They may go large with craft projects like constructing a life-size crocodile on the grounds that both genders will therefore enjoy and access this. These workers try not to provide resources and games that could be construed as stereotypical for boys or girls. In this way they hope to control the amount of stereotypical male or female play behaviour that might manifest itself in a less controlled play setting.

Gender appreciative

Workers here have decided there are differences in boys and girls play. On the whole they operate by creating a gender-neutral environment – let them do what they like – but sometimes they encourage specific events or bring in specific resources that they know will mostly appeal to one gender, e.g. a rap workshop, a dance workshop – hiring in rubber sumo-wrestling suits or bead-making kits. They do this because of their belief in children's rights. These workers believe that in order to enable equality, although they generally do not have any resources or games that are specific to one gender or the other, they occasionally have to offer things that are more stereotypically participated in by either boys or girls.

Gender specific

Workers here very much recognize the differences and regularly try to cater for this by having particular sessions or resources that will mostly appeal to and satisfy one gender. They do this without reinforcing stereotypes and still encourage children to break the mould and be themselves if they wish. They also try to behave in ways that might be considered, by some, to be unexpected for their gender in order to act as role models for the children. These workers try to cater for the potentially different tastes of boys and girls, while supporting children of both genders to participate in any of the play opportunities available: They also role-model alternative gender roles.

We have observed some workers displaying a number of these different ways of intervening related to gender and play, based on the situation at hand and their own level of training, development, personal view and so on; but we have seen many others demonstrating a 'one way suits all' approach. We have run workshops looking at these categories and asking participants to rank them in order of potential effectiveness related to providing an equitable play environment. Interestingly some participants are very capable of recognizing which of the categories they think sound the best and speak very well to the gender agenda, while not necessarily recognizing their own gendered behaviour. Our observations of workers would suggest that by and large most are oblivious of the genderscape of their setting, despite the sometimes definite rhetoric that supports the notion that if you provide the right play environment, all will be equal. Some participants definitely believe that boys will be boys and girls will be girls and that is the natural order of things.

Reflective question

What do you think? If you work with children, which categories seem to genuinely describe your own practice and that of your setting?

Since we developed these categories that describe how we see adults who work with children at play responding to gendered play, we have also become aware of links to two other groupings that relate to gendered behaviour, that we mention here out of interest, because they link to the categories that we have observed. One grouping comes from Kane (2012) and is associated with different ways of parenting in reaction to their children's gendered behaviour and development and the other comes from the Mediterranean Institute of Gender Studies Glossary of Gender Related Terms (2005–9) and is associated with the degree of integration of gender perspectives in any given monitored project as conceptualized in a continuum.

These are as follows:

Kane's 'Parental styles in relation to their children's development of gender'

- **Naturalizers** – these are parents who believe that their children's gender roles are biologically determined and this is not a problem, e.g. parents who sees their son's interest in trucks and building and their daughter's preference for dolls and dance as appropriate.

● **Cultivators** – these are parents who believe that society is the cause of gender differentiation, but they, nevertheless, accept this – when their children behave in gender stereotypical ways they are not concerned.

● **Refiners** – these are parents who believe that gender is a combination of biological and social factors, but they are very concerned about how other people; family, strangers friends etc. perceive the genderedness of their children.

● **Innovators** – these are parents who would like to change the nature of their children's stereotypically gendered roles but follow the path of least resistance.

● **Resisters** – these parents would like to disrupt their children's stereotypical gendered behaviour but are concerned about their children not being accepted in society.

Interestingly, in Kane's interpretation, concern about what others think is not solely related to trying to resist gender stereotypes. And neither Innovators (who are opposing), nor Cultivators (who are promoting) are concerned about judgement – both types clearly think that their parenting in relation to gender is acceptable.

Reflective question

What do you think about these different styles of parenting in relation to gender?

In her research on children, parents and gender nonconformity, Kane (2006) found that parents, by and large, were very happy with their daughters gender non-conformity, such as playing football, building models and displaying some masculine characteristics, but were far less so if their sons showed what are considered to be feminine characteristics, such as, excessive emotionality or passivity and interest in such things as nail polish or Barbie. Kane concluded that most mums and dads actively support their sons' masculinity but had few expectations of femininity in their daughters.

However, Kane also notes that scholars of gender and childhood now see importance in the role of peers in the process of gendering each other, thereby seeing children themselves as active agents rather than merely passive recipients of adult influence.

If we consider these, we can see that gender stereotypes go from being completely reinforced in the first category, through being irrelevant in the second, useful but not challenged in the third, challenged in the fourth and totally challenged in the final category, in pursuit of gender equality.

Table 2 depicts the way that gender perspectives are integrated into proposed projects. Although it is not specifically related to working with children, the categories do seem to mirror some of the categories that we had developed in relation to adults working with children at play and are, therefore, relevant to our theme.

Table 2.

Gender Negative	Gender Neutral	Gender Sensitive	Gender Positive	Gender Transformative
Gender inequalities are reinforced to achieve desired outcomes. Uses gender norms, roles and stereotypes that reinforce gender inequalities	Gender is not considered relevant to development outcomes. Gender norms, roles and relations are not affected (worsened or improved)	Gender is a means to reach set development goals. Addressing gender norms, roles and access to resources in so far as needed to reach project goals	Gender is central to achieving positive development outcomes. Challenging gender norms, roles and access to resources a key component of project outcomes	Gender is central to promoting gender equality and achieving positive development outcomes. Transforming unequal gender relations to promote shared power, control, resources, decision making and support for women's empowerment

Taken from a glossary of gender related terms developed by the Mediterranean Institute for Gender Studies (2005–9: 13–14)

If we link these notions to working with children at play, then we should consider what the aims of organizations that work with children might be and how these may – or may not – be addressing gender.

Neither the new Early Years Educator qualification nor the Level 3 Diploma in Playwork (the industry standard for Early Years and Playwork practitioners in the UK) have any direct mention of gender or sexuality in them. This is an issue that perhaps needs to be revisited. In her doctoral thesis on 'Early Years Practitioners Perceptions of Gender', Mary Wingrave (2014) concludes that gender should be put back on the training agenda in order to give children better fair and equal teaching and learning experiences. The practitioners she interviewed believed, without any theoretical underpinning, that gender affects learning, behaviour and play; and play behaviours in early childhood predict future sexual orientation. These, we believe, are fairly common opinions among many trained and untrained people and while there may be scientists whose research would suggest the same, their work is seldom referred to in relation to common opinion and this common opinion is rebutted by many other scientists who do not believe in biological determinism (see Chapter 4).

All organizations that work with children in the UK will have an Equal Opportunities Policy and this normally includes issues to do with gender and sexuality. This is, however, usually linked in with other aspects of being that are associated with potential inequality, such as class, colour, ability, age, ethnicity and religion. While we see that we cannot lift gender and sexuality out of these contexts, and all of these are equally important, the focus here for us is gender and sexuality. We have seen few separate policies that deal solely with these and few all-inclusive policies that really address these issues in practice. Of course, workers practice is also governed by other policies related to children's welfare, the aims and objectives of the organization and so on. In the field of playwork, workers are required to intervene as little as possible while children are actually playing as the children are considered to be in charge of their own play which has its own benefits. However, we are aware that in more formal or structured settings children's play is carefully motivated, monitored and controlled related to specific developmental outcomes. Workers are often given instructions on how to avoid stereotypical genderscapes and when to intervene in relation to stereotypical gendered behaviour. Worthy as these ideals may be, we wonder firstly whether the environments created are truly non-gendered; secondly how successful the interventions are anyway given the genderscape of children's lives and the weight of genderized behaviour, expectations, images that surround them; and thirdly exactly what type of adult interference is appropriate in relation to gender. Is lip service to an equality agenda really worth it?

It has been suggested that if stereotypically male and female toys/ activities are made available in such a way that boys and girls can play with either (while the workers protect them from any stereotype peer ridicule), some boys will dress up in princess outfits and play with dolls, thereby bringing out their feminine nurturing side, and some girls will play with construction toys thereby developing their spatial relation skills and so forth. But there is no evidence that supports this. Indeed, in a review of 172 studies involving 28,000 children, Lytton and Romney (1991: 109, 267–96) found there was no evidence to support claims that gender-neutral child-rearing had any measurable benefit. They found that 'Boys who are encouraged to play with dolls do not grow up to be any more nurturing than boys who play with trucks or guns'.

Where does this leave us in relation to gender? Do we believe, as Fine (2011: 212) does, that gender is continually emphasized and 'everything around the child indicates that whether one is male or female is a matter of great importance'? If so, should we try and support the status quo – because, as Davies (1989: 238) suggests, in relation to parents, a gender-neutral approach is likely to fail because of the relentless gendering of society: 'Children cannot both be required to position themselves as identifiably male or female and at the same time be deprived of the means of signifying maleness and femaleness.' Or should we support children's struggles to be who they want to be and try to ensure that gender fades into the background of the environments that we provide for them to play in? Eckert and McConnell-Ginet (2003: 23) suggests that 'for some (adults) the maintenance of the gender order is a moral imperative' and for others it is 'a matter of convenience' and it's not worth tampering with!

We leave you here pondering this, while we move on to look more closely at issues to do with how adults respond to children's expressions of sex and sexuality.

Adults response to expressions of sex and sexuality

We suggested above that reflective training on gender should be included in training for all those who work with children. We would also strongly recommend that children's sexuality should be on the training agenda for all professionals working with children. Martinson (1973: 1) says, 'there is probably no human activity about which there is greater curiosity, greater social concern, and less knowledge than sexuality, particularly infant and child sexuality'. 'The child as a subject learning about sexuality and capable of experiencing sexual pleasure doesn't seem to exist in scholarly papers', say Sandfort and Rademakers (2000: 1). There are a few books and websites (see Further Reading) now attempting to address this lack of knowledge and helping both parents and professionals to understand what is normal and healthy sexual behaviour and what might give cause for concern, but these cannot give guaranteed answers – only advise. We will go on to explore a few scenarios to illustrate the complexity of our reactions and responses.

What is our role when we are around playing children and we find them behaving and/or talking in ways we adults would consider 'sexual'? Our first inner prompt (regardless of our emotional response) should be to reflect on what is really happening, rather than making assumptions – as we quoted in the first chapter, 'we do not see things as they are, we see them as *we* are'. Reflection should be our 'default position' all the time when children are playing and is the mark of good practice. But then what? Take the following scenario – what is your own reaction and what would be an appropriate response?

Several children are outside in the adventure playground sitting round a table manipulating lumps of clay. The oldest child is probably about ten and the youngest about six. No one else is close by and the children seem to be unaware of any adult presence. One of the older children starts making a phallic shape and giggling. This prompts similar activity by a couple of other children and soon everyone is giggling. The older child shapes his clay into what looks like an erect phallus and slowly moves his hand up and down it. He is smoothing the clay but also attracting other's attention. He makes a final movement upwards and then raises his hand in an arc saying, 'Whoosh!' The children all laugh and then another child announces he is making sausages and another says, 'I'm doing chips'.

Reflective question

The following are the reactions from playworkers in our workshops: do you identify with any of them?

- Shock – did I really see what I think I saw?
- Panic – I probably should do something but I don't know what
- Concern – what might this mean?
- Anxiety – is this alright or not? – I need to make a decision
- Dread – I really don't want to have to think about or deal with this
- Comfortable – this makes me smile
- Pleased – that children are free to express themselves
- Neutral – seems normal – doesn't provoke any reaction in me

Having established our first reaction (and in practice gained some control over our feelings and recognition that they may not be representative of the real situation), what might – or should – our response be? Here are some possibilities (there are bound to be more).

- Turn a blind eye and move away

- Do something else/distract with a new idea

- Move closer to distract by sheer presence

- Continue to observe and listen (unobtrusively)

- Ask what they are playing/doing

- Ask what they were laughing about

- Ignore the whole scenario

- Decide to monitor closely from now on – the older child in particular

- Have a word with the older child about behaving inappropriately

- Ask the older child what he was doing

- Stop any further sexual play/behaviour/language

- Say nothing to the children but discuss what you have seen with colleagues

- Say nothing but record the incident

If your response engendered reactions, conversation or questions from any of the children, would you:

- Refer children to relevant books/literature about sex that children can dip into or read

- Encourage honesty/open conversation/questions?

- Use their language?

- Answer their questions honestly?

- Give them further information?

- Tell parents what has taken place?

- Tell them to take their questions to their parents?

- Change the subject?

There is of course no one right answer, although some reactions and responses will be more helpful than others. Every situation is different, every child is unique and no textbook can tell us definitively what do. Which of these responses might be appropriate at different times will of course depend on what is happening. But the assessment of 'what is *really* happening?' is absolutely crucial in informing us what to say or do (or not say and do) next.

So, what might be really happening in this scenario and how might we know? Is the older boy really shaping a penis – he may or may not be, but it's perhaps more likely that he is. Are the other children who copy him also shaping penises or are some making sausages (one certainly is!)? They may or may not be. Is the older boy showing an awareness of masturbation? Is he showing knowledge of orgasm or is he making a flourished pronunciation of his clay creation? If it is the former, how does he know this? Has he experienced it (we do know it is possible at his age) or has he seen it happen in someone else? If it is the latter, was that a playful, an inappropriate or an abusive scenario: was it real or was it virtual? And – probably the million dollar question – has this enactment or re-enactment caused harm to him or to any of the other children who are rolling clay? Would any of the younger children necessarily have known what he might have been doing (and if so, does that matter)?

These kinds of questions – which cannot all be answered – are the core of reflective practice. We need to see these situations through children's eyes. Looking through an adult lens and making assumptions will lead to unhelpful interventions. Certainly blaming, judging and scolding children will only achieve humiliation and confusion. If we are uncomfortable and concerned, we have to know why – is it a reaction in ourselves that may be clouding our judgement. Understanding that children are sexual beings and how they are likely to develop sexually as they grow is an essential tool – as is knowing what kind of behaviours really are cause for concern (we will look at these in the next chapter). But recognizing, examining and moving past our first reactions are every bit as important if we are to truly support children.

Read the following scenarios and consider what your reactions and responses might be.

> There are a dozen or so children in the school playground at the after-school club. Two children – a boy and a girl, aged about ten – have their arms round each other and have their mouths glued to each other. The other children who are all aged between eight and eleven, are calling out comments like 'ugh what do you taste like?!', 'yeah, keep on going!', 'we can see everything you're doing!' and 'whoohoo, go for it!'. While this is happening, one of the older children is organizing the others into collecting soft play blocks and large pieces of material and putting them just inside the large concrete tunnel in the playground and the 'couple' are shepherded towards the tunnel with comments like 'you'll be alright now' and 'we've made you a bed' etc. The girl and boy do not protest and crawl into the tunnel laughing.

On an afternoon during playscheme, all the workers and children have gone to the local park which has a play area with fixed play equipment, woods and fields. Most of the children are off playing tracking and there are just a few older children (10–12) left on the play area. The playworkers are ranging around the park, observing and supporting the children's play where needed. One worker comes over to the play area unnoticed by the children there and she sees a group of five – mostly boys – up on the 'bridge' between a slide and a ramp standing around a boy and girl lying down. The boy is on top of the girl and they seem to be simulating sexual intercourse. The boys are all laughing and the girl is smiling. No other children are in the immediate vicinity.

Reflective questions

Again – what is your initial reaction and how might you respond? Where do we stand on all this? What are our attitudes and our approach? Are we:

- Permissive?
- Supportive?
- Restrictive?
- Repressive?

What about those of us who work with children and young people who are post-pubescent with more knowledge about sexual matters and perhaps some sexual experience? Might there be different considerations and possible responses? Children in this age group are still curious, still developing and still exploring although we – and they – need to be aware that their hormones are now an added driver, often precipitating active experimentation with the additional possibility of pregnancy. What is our role with this age group? Might it be to:

- Give advice?
- Give/stock information? – e.g. books, leaflets etc.
- Take them to clinics?
- Liaise with parents?
- Listen?

- Discuss concerns and/or situations with them?

- Discuss concerns and/or situations with colleagues?

- Do nothing?

- Stop or discourage any sexual behaviour?

- Supply with condoms?

- Encourage debate?

- Signpost to websites/info/clinics?

- Record concerns?

- Eavesdrop?

- Tell them about your own experiences?

Which of the above might be most appropriate in the following situation described to us? Once again, note your first reaction before you decide.

An adventure playground caters for teenagers from thirteen to eighteen during some weekday evenings and is staffed by a mixture of playworkers and youth workers. There are a number of wooden ramps and structures, nooks and crannies on the site and one of the workers became aware during one session that one area underneath a wooden platform that was fenced on three sides often had a couple of young people inside it with a third person just outside. Couples came and went and the person outside also varied. The worker thought the person outside was acting as a look-out (as others were stopped from going in) and suspected that there was probably some kind of sexual behaviour going on inside.

Our response will of course vary according to the situation in hand and according to our professional role – many youth workers and/or youth counsellors with additional training in sexual health and/or education do regularly engage in conversations with young people about safe sex and contraception, whereas playworkers and teachers are not expected to do so and are certainly not equipped to do so in their training. But whatever our role we all do need to identify and move past our first reactions in order to be more objective. The reflective tool 'IMEE' that was originally developed for playworkers (Hughes 1996a) would be useful here to help us consider what we feel, know, experience and have learnt. 'IMEE' symbolizes intuition, memory, experience and evidence and is explained and adapted to our current inquiry.

Reflective practice – IMEE

Intuition

This is our unique internal judgement, a gut feeling, which is not necessarily based on evidence or what we know or have been taught, but how we instinctively feel/think. Our intuition may differ to that of others. We will therefore have an intuitive response to children's sexual play/behaviour.

Memory

This constitutes what we remember of our own childhood experiences connected with sex and/or sexuality: where we were, what we were doing, who we were with, etc and how we felt at that time. These memories affect our reactions in the present.

Experience

Our experience of living and/or working with children and what this has taught us about children – what they usually like and dislike, what they may or may not need, how they do and don't behave, and what works best for them in terms of our interventions or strategies etc. Such experience contributes to our judgements of a current scenario.

Evidence

This comprises the related literature and research that informs our interpretation of circumstances now. This should of course include what is most recent – more is being researched and written all the time and needs to be read, digested, reflected on, thought critically about, tested and used as evidence where this is appropriate. For interpreting sexual play behaviours – such evidence should include research and literature on play itself as well as on sexuality and sexual development.

There are of course pros and cons to each of these – bad memories or past negative experiences can make us over-react or assume things now; our evidential understanding may be biased or not up to date; our experience may be narrow or sheltered, etc.

Reflective question

Can you think of specific examples yourself in how using all of these – your intuition, your memory, your experience and evidence you have heard or read – can be either constructive and/or unhelpful in assessing a present situation.

Taken together, using all four 'IMEE' categories in the here and now helps us be both human and objective and brings all our related feelings, thoughts, experience and knowledge to the surface to assist us in questioning and ultimately interpreting what is happening now. Considering all four of these – for they sometimes contradict each other – will lead us to understand both ourselves and children better and to make more informed judgements about what we see and hear.

Reflective questions

Can you apply each of these categories to the scenarios we have given? What is your intuitive response in each case? What memories might they stir and are these positive or not? What experiences of children have you had as an adult that are relevant here? What evidence and/or research about play and about children's sexuality have you come across that informs your thinking about these scenarios?

We are conscious that in all these scenarios – all of which were real life examples – we have concentrated on our personal thoughts and feelings. We have not explored the differences between natural and healthy sexual behaviours and those which might give us cause for concern – these differences of course fit into the 'evidence category' of IMEE as they help us know when intervention might be called for. We will give an overview of these differences in the next chapter and references for further information.

We are now moving on to our final chapter, which will explore the wider implications for practice in a range of settings where children play and learn. It will examine how we can better recognize and support children's developing sense of gender and emerging sexuality and all that might mean in terms of staff development and training, policy and procedures, resources, communication with adults, professionals, parents and children, and most importantly our interventions with children themselves.

Suggested reading

Hughes, B. (2011), *Evolutionary Playwork*, London: Routledge.

Jones, P. (2009), *Rethinking Childhood: Attitudes in Contemporary Society*, London: Continuum.

Martin, K. (2005), 'William Wants a Doll. Can he have One? Feminists, Childcare Advisors and Gender Neutral Childrearing', *Gender and Society* 19 (4): 456–79.

Padawer, Ruth (2012), 'What's so Bad About a Boy Who Wants to Wear a Dress?' *New York Times*, 8 August. Available online: http://www.nytimes.com/2012/08/12/magazine/whats-so-bad-about-a-boy-who-wants-to-wear-a-dress.html?pagewanted=all&_r=0 (accessed 25 June 2015).

CHAPTER SEVEN

Conscious competence in support of children playing

Introduction

This is the chapter in which we bring everything together and make final applications to practice of the ideas we have explored. The reality is that our thoughts, feelings and beliefs about play and gender and sexuality within childhood, will impact on our practice – on what we do and say and it will also impact on how children feel and behave. We give below a list of places that are, or may be, staffed by adults, where children should have some time to play freely in their own way and according to their own ideas. Do you work in any of these, or are you a parent or carer?

- Primary schools
- Secondary schools
- Nursery schools
- Playgroups
- Children's centres
- Creches
- Before and/or after-school provision
- Holiday clubs and playschemes
- Uniformed organizations
- Parks or recreation grounds, fixed public playgrounds
- Hospital wards or clinics
- Youth clubs and youth centres
- Children's specialist clubs

The people who work in any of the above settings could, therefore, comprise:

- Teachers
- Teaching assistants
- Youth workers
- Playworkers
- Early years workers
- Hospital play specialists
- Childminders
- Lunchtime supervisors
- Sports coaches
- Play rangers
- Playleaders
- Community workers/community development workers
- Volunteers

Are you represented here?

While some on the above list may not have play as their primary focus, they are still often present when children are playing and oversee what goes on. Parents and carers too, are also supervisors of playing children.

Whether supporting self-directed play is or is not a major part of our job, we all have a responsibility to cultivate an understanding of it as it will surely enhance our relationship with and comprehension of children and it can definitely inform and complement other areas of our professional role. When it comes to children's developing sense of gender and sexuality – both of which are naturally and regularly expressed in their playing, we would all do well to pay heed to such playing for its fundamental contribution to their present and future health and well-being. Recognizing and understanding what we see and hear of their play and knowing whether, when and why we may need to respond to their play, are essential skills for any adult.

We have explored in this book, theories and constructs about play, gender and sexuality to help us all – parents and professionals – to think critically about how these may impact on children and to especially help us to consider our own attitudes and approach to children, who continue to play out their queries and findings with such natural dedication.

With regard to children's growth and their sexual development in particular, it might be helpful to have an overview of what might be expected or typical of children at different ages. This does come with a warning however, because all children are unique and members of different families, diverse cultures and a range of social environments all of which impacts for better or worse on their thoughts, feelings, abilities and opportunities. As Parsons said, 'the expression of sexuality in children varies as a function of culture, gender and the individual' (1983: 38). We cannot and should not fit children into boxes. Nevertheless if we proceed with caution, a general survey (we have described it as 'normative') can be useful and we give this below, amalgamated from a range of sources and our observations.

'Normative' sexual behaviours from birth to puberty

0–1 years

- Spontaneous reflexive penile erection/vaginal lubrication.
- Sensual pleasure from being caressed and from sucking.
- Explores body and genitals during nappy changing and bathing.
- Enjoys nudity.

1–3 years

- Occasional masturbation.
- Interest in own excretions.
- Seeks and gives physical affection.
- Shows playful interest in other's genitals, especially those of another gender.
- Continues to enjoy nudity.
- Recognition of different genders (although often by hair or clothing).
- Interest in words for body parts.
- Boys realize they can cause erections.

3–5 years

- Tries to touch or shows interest in other children's genitals.
- Tries to touch or shows interest in breasts, bottoms or genitals of adults.
- Asks questions about breasts and body parts and their purpose.
- Role-play games, e.g. mummies and daddies, doctors and nurses.
- Touches/rubs own genitals when going to sleep, when excited, scared or anxious.
- Explores differences between males and females, boys and girls.
- Has erections.
- Interested in watching people doing bathroom functions, washing etc.
- Interested in having/bathing a baby.
- May put something in the genitals or rectum for curiosity or exploration.
- Uses 'dirty' or slang words for bodily functions and body parts – often with great humour.

5–8 years

- Curiosity-based sex play with same and opposite sex friends, increasingly in private.
- Use of slang words to describe body parts and sexuality.
- Starting to show a desire for personal privacy and an interest in boundaries.
- Decrease in public masturbation, but may increase in private and may be more pleasure focussed than comfort
- Asking questions about sexual activity and reproduction and wanting to understand
- Asking questions about gender and gender roles
- Telling dirty jokes and using swear words
- When playing generally, this is mostly in same-sex groups

- Children tease each other for behaving like the opposite gender
- Imitating gender roles

9–12 years

- Continuation of curiosity-based sex play with same and opposite sex friends, although increasing sexual knowledge may make this more experimental and intimate
- Playing gender roles with less rigidity
- Testosterone and oestrogen begin to be produced and bodies begin to change – this happens earlier for girls.
- Menstruation may begin for girls.
- Nocturnal emission may begin for boys
- Spontaneous erections start to increase for boys
- Wanting personal privacy
- Increased use of mobile phones and internet – browsing and sharing sexual images and information.
- Experience of first major crush
- Wanting and talking about having boyfriends or girlfriends and who they 'fancy'
- Masturbation in private increases
- Anxiety over how to behave and/or flirt with opposite sex – testing out sexual scripts
- Anxiety over 'am I "normal"'
- Interest in romance
- Increase in erotic impulses
- Increasingly preoccupied with own body

To repeat the warning – this does not mean all children will demonstrate or experience all of these, nor does it mean that they may be regularly and consistently seen in any one child. These are examples of healthy unrepressed children naturally expressing their curiosity about themselves and others from time to time as they grow up. Sexual play and genderized play are the means by which children explore themselves and their world and make sense of it all – as they do with all other kinds of playing.

A possible cause for concern

Some of the above behaviours however, may give us cause for concern if they are obsessive or compulsive – as Rich (2012: 1) comments:

> The normative behaviours of childhood and adolescence are of concern when they are extensive or suggest preoccupation, or involve others in ways that are not consensual. Sexual behaviours in children present a special concern when they appear as prominent features in a child's life, or when sexual play or behaviours are not welcomed by other children involved in the play.

There are other behaviours too, that need sensitive monitoring and possible intervention. Time and space does not permit here to explore all of these; indeed others have done so – Cavanagh-Johnson (2013), Brennan and Graham (2012) – but we can make brief reference to these.

Some children may have been exposed to sexual images, acts and/or conversation – this may be by simply watching soaps regularly, or it may be by having access to adult films, being present when adults are having sex, listening to adult conversation, seeing adult material. Such exposure could be unintentional or due to ignorance on the part of the child's carer, or it could be deliberate. Some children may have been touched inappropriately by older children, teenagers or adults and this may have happened once, a few or many times. Some children may come from homes where there is neglect, domestic violence and/or great stress. These represent a very wide range of possible experience in a child's life, but in order to make sense of what they have seen, heard or been involved in, many children may well 'play this out'. For some children this may manifest itself in initiating sexual play with others – still with their consent, but perhaps more often and with greater seriousness than another child. For some children, they may manipulate other children into sexual play. For others, they may coerce or force other children into sexual behaviour. All of the children on this spectrum of possible sexual behaviours are showing signs of minor through to major disturbance and need sensitive intervention and even therapy to help them in their present life and to ensure that this does not evolve into future offending behaviour.

If children manifest the following, there is cause for concern while recognizing that there may be multiple causes, i.e., these do not necessarily mean the child has been sexually abused. Many things can prompt questionable sexual behaviours in children and equally so, many children who have been sexually abused, show no such symptoms (Drach et al. 2001). Family adversity, violence and/or how power is demonstrated in the home, family and cultural boundaries regarding 'appropriate' physical and sexual behaviour, attachment issues – all these can influence a child's sexual behaviour. Cavanagh-Johnson (1991: 8) wisely cautions us:

There is no single standard for determining normal sexual behaviours in all children, since there are individual differences due to the developmental level of the child and due to the amount of exposure the child has had to adult sexuality, nudity, explicit television and videos [...] The sexual behaviours of a child represent only part of their total being. Sexual behaviours should not be used as the sole criteria for determining whether a child has a significant problem.

Behaviours giving cause for concern

- Preoccupation with sexual play

- Showing knowledge of sex usually considered beyond their age

- Inability to stop engaging in sexual play after being asked to stop

- Hurting or causing discomfort to other children through sexual play/activities

- Approaching and initiating sexual activity with much younger or much older children and even adults

- Using threats or tricking other children into sexual play or activity

- Engaging in sexual activity with animals

- Little recognition of boundaries or the rights of others

- Complaints from children about another's child's sexual behaviour

Family Planning Queensland have produced what they call a traffic light framework, (Brennan and Graham 2012) to identify behaviours that are healthy (green), behaviours to be concerned about (amber) and behaviours that are problematic or harmful (red). This framework has been adopted and adapted by Brook Young People and The Lucy Faithfull Foundation for use by parents and professionals in the UK and Ireland and readers might find these helpful (see suggested reading at the end of the chapter). Cavanagh-Johnson (2013) has also developed a useful continuum listing many characteristics that help us understand children's sexual behaviours; namely:

- **Group 1 – Natural and healthy sexual play** – children who periodically and voluntarily play with their peers as a way to satisfy their curiosity about gender and bodies.

- **Group 2 – Sexually reactive behaviours** – children who have been exposed to sexual stimuli in some way and are working out their confusion and what this means by personally regularly behaving in sexual ways that are not secret and not manipulative of others.

● **Group 3 – Extensive mutual sexual behaviours** – children who regularly use the full range of adult sexual activity as a way to emotionally relate to their peers and try to keep this secret – they manipulate but do not force others into this.

● **Group 4 – Molestation behaviour** – children who impulsively and aggressively coerce others into sexual activity with little sympathy for their victims. These children will almost certainly have been abused in some way themselves and children in both groups 3 and 4 will need specialist help to understand and change their behaviour.

We do need to learn to know – in practice – the difference between healthy and unhealthy sexual behaviours in children. However, our intention here is not to focus on the problematic but to develop a greater awareness and acceptance of what is natural and healthy sexual play that is often as much about understanding gender as it is about understanding sexuality.

Healthy gender play – is there such a thing?

We, as adults, rarely have the same knee jerk reactions about our children's gender expression through play that we have about their sexual expression and yet if some researchers are to be believed, children playing out their gendered scripts may have lasting consequences for their ongoing and future life choices, opportunities for personal expression, emotional wellbeing and in some cases even their morality. It is impossible to talk about 'normative' gender behaviour, as there is no such thing, although some parents and carers express concerns if their children do not conform to gender stereotypes and some actively work, either knowingly or unknowingly, to ensure that their children either do or don't conform, as they consider either one of these 'healthy' depending upon what they feel the most appropriate 'lasting consequences' might be for children. Some parents and scientists believe that girls should be girls and boys should be boys and that is in their best interests and some think that girls and more recently boys are poorly served if they are confined to stereotypical gender roles. Through play children express their whole being across the spectrum of that which we describe as gender and who they are and how they play will be prompted by many things including: the environment in which they live and play; the resources that are available; their own DNA and personality; who their friends are; who they play with and the gender role models in their lives.

The majority of adults seem to have their views about whether boys and girls are different and behave differently, which they stick to and thus play out the associated adult role without further thought. What are our responsibilities here? Should we leave children prey to the gender pressures that living in any society brings and leave them to develop in whatever way this leads them? Should we try to manipulate things and provide what we consider to be an appropriately non-gendered environment, resources, play opportunities and so on and leave them to make of it what they will? Should we provide a wide range of knowingly gendered and gender-neutral play resources and opportunities and let them choose? Should we strictly monitor their every move and ensure that they never behave in stereo-typically gendered ways or play with stereotypically gendered resources? Should we take pride in their gender expressions and help them to navigate the joys and sorrows of being either male or female? Should we ensure that we role model non-gendered attitudes and behaviours so that they are able to realize that men and women are able to do the same things? Or should we just behave in whatever way seems natural to us and let the consequences for children take care of themselves? It depends how we view gender issues and whether we think that we have any part in children's expressions of gender.

Various concerns have been raised throughout this book about whether gender and sex are mainly a biological or sociological manifestation of life. We think that we can safely say that both seem to come into it, but academics from opposing camps have difficulty accepting alternative viewpoints. There are also very present concerns about how 'the wallpaper of children's lives' (gender and sex) is potentially having damaging effects on them, now and in the future. Whether this is the case is very difficult for us to know as we live in the present, in the world that we have been a part of creating and some of the concern seems to hark back to an imagined golden past, or envisage an imagined golden future where all people will be equal and where issues to do with sex and gender will not trouble children growing up. Below we list some of the concerns that have been voiced throughout the book that we have delved into but about which we have reached no static conclusions.

Concerns voiced in the book

● Many people, particularly women, are disadvantaged by the gender role they play out in our society and play has a relationship to this.

● Society is becoming increasingly sexualized and genderized and this is affecting children's development in a negative way.

● Stereotypical expectations related to the behaviour of sons and daughters puts them under pressure to conform and this includes

what toys they play with, what games they play and what clothes
they wear.

● Parents and their gender biases cause children to grow up in
particular ways.

● Girls should be girls and boys should be boys and we shouldn't
interfere – it's a biological fact.

● If gendered behaviour is biologically determined it perpetuates
inequality.

● Genderized play has significance for mental health, social
relationships and cognition across the life span.

● Through gendered play, the environments that children inhabit are
changed and subsequently, because of this, the lives of girls and
boys are differently channelled, constrained or expanded.

● Cross-gender play in childhood might be a sign of homosexuality in
adulthood.

● An assumption of heteronormativity disadvantages children and
their growing sexuality and particularly those who do not fit into
that assumption.

● The differences between boys and girls has been greatly exaggerated
– there are far more similarities than differences and this is not
acknowledged properly.

● There seems to be huge emotional investment and interest in either
proving or disproving gender differences – why bother?

● We need to be aware of boy-girl differences so we can help
children compensate for these early on, allowing every child to
flourish in his or her strengths, but always looking for opportunities
to stretch them in ways that their peers and the broader culture will
not.

● Children are seen as being disadvantaged by age, social status and
powerlessness and this can in turn make them disadvantaged by
being seen as victims of life rather than actors in life.

● Unconscious gender stereotyping and talking of all children as being
the same is a problem. All children are unique.

These concerns are a small snapshot of the concerns that some parents,
carers, academics, scientists, children's workforce, the public and politicians have related to the 'genderization of childhood', while many more are
prepared to accept the status quo: what is – is!

Play deprivation and play bias

So what would 'healthy gender play' and a 'healthy gender play environment' be? We think the environment would be like any wonderful play environment as follows:

- rich in sensory possibilities of sight, sound, smell, taste and touch.

- access to both indoors and outdoors.

- access to the elements – earth, air, fire and water.

- possibilities for all the play types.

- rich in variety of lose parts and different sorts of resources.

- adaptable and transformable.

- un-adulterated.

And within this type of environment, and without the adulterative interventions of adults, children's 'healthy gender play' would be whatever is played – sometimes gendered, sometimes not.

In his commentary on the genesis of playwork, Hughes (2012: 36) talks of concerns during the late 1980s that maybe 'female children' weren't getting enough out of the adventure playground environment, and special 'girls only' sessions and activities were tried. These were not very successful and the question was asked:

> Can playwork identify play experiences that apply specifically to female children, and by offering them ensure that girls are as protected as boys against play deprivation, or should we assume that an enriched play space that incorporated the spirit of, for example, the playwork menu, would provide an appropriate play backdrop for girls and boys?

The answers that were discussed then were as follows:

- Adult culture is irrelevant in the play setting – the culture is created by the children.

- That sort of level of intervention would be adulterative.

- The play needs of all children (boys and girls), irrespective of parental background are always the same, give or take some emphasis.

FIGURE 7.1 My *den*
Permission granted by Baker

Do you agree with these answers and if not, what would your answers be?

These answers would seem to fly in the face of those people that believe that we can somehow manipulate children's emerging expressions of gender by offering play experiences and environments in a particular gendered or non-gendered way. However, what perhaps does become more significant, are the issues of play stimulus, play deprivation and play bias. These notions work on the principle that all children need environmental stimulation (as above) with a balance between both positive and negative stimuli and an over-or-under bias in any direction will result in either problem or biased behaviour in the play environment and possibly play deprivation. This, Hughes (2012: 37) proposes, may in turn lead to diminished ability in various areas of development such as communication, creativity, problem solving or socializing (and we would like to add unbiased gender development). If the environment and resources available for play are very limited, children may not be motivated to play across all play types (see Appendix B) or indeed if the environment and resources are very biased in a particular direction. For instance, if everything is very stereotypically 'girly' or 'boyish', then children may be mainly motivated to play in particular ways that suit the environment and resources available, but possibly not themselves, thereby creating limits on their play and all that is possibly attendant with that. For us, this leads away from seeing gender as an isolated issue, but one of many, and play environments and resources plus the interventions of adults into play, as being the main issue.

Hughes (2012: 66/67) talks of sexual activity as being instinctive and the need for some sort of sexual interaction to occur as children are growing up so that they are not emotionally or physically disadvantaged, but how children get their experience is 'vexing' to adults. He wonders whether playworkers (but we would add all adults) should 'let it happen, pretend it isn't happening; turn a blind eye or prohibit it?' We would also include the playing out of gender roles here. Children need to practice themselves in order to understand themselves.

Conscious competence

Returning to ourselves then, for we are the adults around playing children, how competent are we – or do we perceive ourselves to be – when observing and responding to children's gendered and/or sexual play?

The 'Conscious Competence' model Broadwell (1969) is useful here as illustrated in Figure 7.2.

If we relate the model to our subject, it begins in the first quadrant with those who react and respond to children's gendered and sexual play without thinking; making assumptions and judgements about what they see and hear based on their own biased feelings, values and untested knowledge to date. Such responses are often negative and usually repressive in that they do not see from a child's perspective, nor affirm or support healthy play. Anyone who is operating in this quadrant is completely unaware that their practice needs consideration and change.

The second quadrant includes those who have moved on and have read something, observed another practitioner or listened to an alternative perspective that has made them question themselves and realize that their approach is unhelpful and uninformed. They therefore seek to know more,

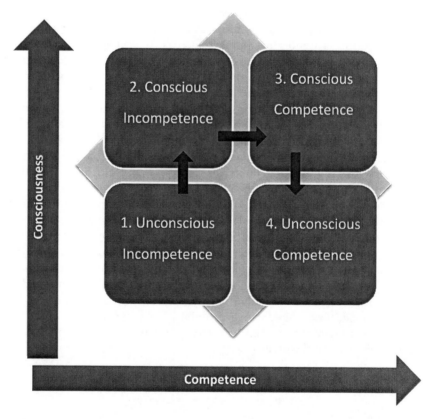

FIGURE 7.2 *Conscious competence model. Although this is our illustration, it is based on a model widely used on scores of websites. The originator of the matrix diagram is unknown however, although the earliest content seems to be attributed to Broadwell (1969).*

critically analyse and reflect on this knowledge, apply it to their own practice and begin to change their responses.

The third quadrant depicts those who have and are changing their attitudes and behaviours to understand and better support children and to see the world through their eyes. These people consciously and regularly question themselves and what they see and hear.

The fourth quadrant houses those few people who have become so adept at genuine and constant reflective practice (through models like IMEE explored in the previous chapter) that their observations and reactions to individual children are finely honed to be naturally understanding and supportive.

Where are we in relation to play, gender and/or children's sexuality?

- Unconsciously incompetent?

- Consciously incompetent?

- Consciously competent?

- Unconsciously competent?

Reflective questions

Which quadrant 'fits' you and your practice regarding play? Regarding gender? Regarding sexuality?

We would suggest that anyone who has read this book with an open mind would site themselves in the second or third quadrants – perhaps moving from one to the other in different situations. Despite our own research, accumulated knowledge and years of practice, even we would not place ourselves in the fourth quadrant. Such sensitivity to children and their playing is hard-earned with honesty, humility and ongoing critical thinking and deep reflection. Are enough of us – as parents or professionals – getting sufficient input and mentoring to at least get us into the second quadrant and hopefully beyond?

At this point it might help us if we return now to three aspects we have already explored in previous chapters and from which we have formed our 'recommendations for practice', which we expound in the afterword. These are:

1 Our four categories of the differing views that academics have related to theories about gender in Chapter 4 (pp. 73–9).

2 Our types of responses to gendered and genderized play in Chapter 6 (pp. 131–3).

3 Our initial areas of interest in Chapter 1 (pp. 4–5).

1. Categories of differing views

We categorized all the expressed views about sex differences in Table 1 (Chapter 4) and simplify them here. Category A comprised those who believe there are many definite hard-wired differences between boys and girls. Category B incorporated those who believe there are only a very few innate differences that are compounded and exacerbated by societal expectations. Category C included those who believe there are no proven differences at all. Out of these first three categories, having sifted through all the evidence, we find ourselves agreeing mostly with Category B. However we feel the fourth category D is the most important because rather than trying to prove the causes of gender differences this category concentrates on recognizing and responding to children and young people who are forming their gender identities here and now. We are far more interested in observing and thinking about our response to children playing in the present because we are interested in ensuring that no boy or girl is limited by their play environment and experience. We believe there are some types of responses that will better support children's play and some that will not and we outline the latter below.

2. Types of responses

Depending upon the circumstances that prevail at any setting where children play, different types of responses may be relevant at different times (see Chapter 6). However there are some types of adulterative or lazy responses or interventions that can lead to either severe limitations in the play environment and/or stereotypical responses to girls and boys playing and we tend to feel these should be avoided. From our own list of observed responses, those to *avoid* are:

- Gender similar – this category of worker tries to deny the existence of any potential innate differences in the play of boys and girls and leaves out any resources that could be classed as stereotypical for either boys or girls, thereby limiting the depth of play opportunities available to all the children.

- Gender stereotyped – this category of worker caters very specifically for girls with resources and games specifically considered appropriate for females and for boys with things that are specifically considered suitable for males thereby limiting the play choices and potential of both boys and girls.

- Gender controlled – workers in this category dislike any evidence of stereotyped gender play and try to influence the development of boys and girls by intervening in almost every aspect of the environment, resources and play behaviours thereby adulterating the total play experience.

● Gender ignorant – this category of worker does not ever think about issues to do with gender. They have no new thoughts about the potential differences or similarities between the play of boys and girls and just respond in the way that comes naturally to them, whatever that may be. Therefore children may or may not be subject to any interventions associated with the other categories, but this will be by chance rather than from consideration.

Reflective questions

Are there other responses or interventions that you are aware of that may be equally unhelpful and therefore should be avoided?

3. Initial questions

And finally we look back to where we started in Chapter 1, where we stated that we were interested in:

● the everyday experiences of girls and boys, whether there are differences and what might be the cause of these;

● how children play in response to these if there are differences;

● whether children's play culture impacts on their current and future lives; and

● whether adult responses to children's genderized and sexualized playing helps or hinders children and society.

We have explored the differences between boys and girls and their lived experience, particularly of play, by looking at the conclusions, views and anecdotal evidence of others related to gender and sexuality; by reflecting on our own experiences of working with and observing children at play and by analysing this against the professional conclusions of others and the views of children, parents, carers and children's workers.

We believe that we have shown that, regardless of what adults think, most boys and girls do consider themselves to be different and that, for the majority of boys and girls, their everyday experiences are different, partly due to adult intervention and partly due to their own behaviour.

The reasons for these differences are many and varied and hotly disputed by different sectors of the scientific community, but it has probably always been so in most parts of the world. We live in a patriarchal world that has been dominated by men for centuries but is slowly changing in some aspects. Attempts at change in order to bring about greater equality between males and females may have different goals for the different sexes, different cultures, different societies and for different families. There is a long way to go in relation to equality of the sexes and for people across the spectrum of sexuality and where exactly we want to get to is not agreed by all. How to get to wherever it is we think we are going is not simple or desired by all people. Some people are perfectly happy with the way the gendered world is and want to keep to the status quo and children have to navigate their way through these different adult ideologies. We as people interested in children at play, should be mindful of the varying views about gender and sexuality that society holds so that we do not try to impose our own view on the play environment.

We have tried to show that the responses of boys and girls to their world are also shaped by the world's response to them. Children have their own agency, their own culture and they affect their world as much as they are affected by it. The play of boys and girls can be seen to be very different at different ages, stages and in different contexts; however these differences are not set in stone, whether they are real or constructed and play like all of life is not one static thing it is many and varied – it always depends upon the circumstances!

We have looked at the notion that children's play culture impacts on their current and future lives in relation to their gender and sexuality and we believe we can safely say that all forms of play feature highly in children's current lives. At different times playing with their sexuality is children's way of finding out about their sexual selves and gender issues are an ever-present overlay on their play. These two aspects of play will feature more or less prominently depending upon the circumstances, throughout their lives. Whether gendered and genderized play has any more signifi-cance than any other part of a child's life on their future outcomes is very difficult to ascertain. There are so many variables that have to be taken into account, which we believe is why no scientists or academics have been able to conclusively agree, whether or why there are real differences between the play of boys and girls. However we are certain that play is very important for boys and girls for many reasons some of these being as Hughes (2012: 66) lists, it enables children to:

● Think for themselves

● Make their own decisions

● Have confidence in their own abilities

- Develop empathy
- Develop personal values
- Test out strategies without the stigma of failure
- Resolve contradictions and inconsistencies
- Communicate their needs, beliefs and desires more clearly
- Have an understanding of the life process
- Develop understanding of the interrelationship of everything
- Question everything

And this includes playing with their own and others' sexuality, their own gender identity and their own and others' gender roles.

Play, sexuality and gender are all complex subjects that are debated and researched by adults, but also experienced in the everyday lives of children and young people. We have explored the evidence and posed many questions throughout the book, which we hope will prompt your own reflection and thinking and enable us all to become more consciously competent when we are around children playing. In Chapter 1, we said that

FIGURE 7.3 *This is* our *world*
Permission granted by Peach and Walker

although we are unable to come up with any hard conclusions, we have been able to develop some recommendations based on our research, our practice, our experiences and observations. We will explain and share these with you in our afterword.

Suggested Reading

Brook (n.d.), 'Sexual Behaviours Traffic Light Tool'. Available online: http://www.brook.org.uk/old/index.php/traffic-light-tool-0-to-5 (accessed 19 May 2015).

Cavanagh-Johnson, T. (2013), *Understanding Children's Sexual Behaviours*, San Diego: Institute on Violence, Abuse and Trauma.

Hughes, B. (2012), *Evolutionary Playwork Second Edition*, London: Routledge.

Parents Protect (2010+), 'Project of The Lucy Faithfull Foundation'. Available online: http://www.parentsprotect.co.uk/ (accessed 19 August 2015).

Stop it Now UK & Ireland (n.d.), 'Project of The Lucy Faithfull Foundation'. Available online: http://www.stopitnow.org.uk/ (accessed 19 May 2015).

AFTERWORD

This book has been a long time in the making and as we described in Chapter 1, we set out to be open-minded and not to try and prove any particular standpoints. This doesn't mean we haven't held or expressed our own views from time to time, although we have both shifted our thinking on a number of occasions on aspects of gender and sexuality. We would be lying, however, if we did not state that we have not changed our minds at all about championing children's right to play in their own way for their own reasons. We, therefore, feel it is only right to set out what at this point we feel are positive approaches and responses to children playing – this applies to all their playing as well as when they are expressing, questioning and playfully exploring their sexuality and gender.

While experience has taught us to not be static or entrenched and we have both had Eureka moments at different times that have demolished a number of prior dearly held principles, we have, nevertheless, thought a lot about what we might call good practice. We set out here our underlying beliefs and then offer our current recommendations for practice:

We believe that play features highly in children's lives and is essential for their well-being

All adults would do well to recognize this and ensure that children have time and space to play without adult censorship and interference. There are plenty of books out there that focus on the power of adults to reduce stereotypical thinking in children by giving them toys normally associated with the opposite gender and encouraging boys and girls to play together and so on. There is some truth here – we would agree with widening children's horizons and, when relevant, having conversations with children that counteract the deluge of stereotypical ideas and behaviours that assail all children through books, toys, the media and other people. 'Other people' would include us, too, as we may all unconsciously be giving out similar messages about who boys and girls are, what they like and how they behave. However, many of the books that aim to help adults adjust children's gender stereotypical behaviour have misunderstood two things; one is that children learn just as much if not more from each other than they do from their parents, carers, teachers, etc., and the second is that play is the medium through which children naturally work a lot of this stuff out for themselves and we should not underestimate their ability to do so. Children do often segregate into like-gender groups – considering the genderscaped background of their early years it would be unsurprising if they didn't, but we often fail to understand that this segregation is one aspect of the process of their gender identity formation. Young children have 'an emotional investment in getting their gendered behaviour correct' (Martin 2011: 133), but as they grow they do a lot of varied borderwork and test out gendered ideas in their playing. Similarly, considering the way that the adult world 'treats, recognises, regulates, punishes and ultimately creates children's sexualities [… we] should attend equally to the ways in which children are active in this process and produce their own sexual identities, cultures and relations' (Renold 2005: 22). Ultimately, children are on their own journey and we can support them and be a positive influence, but we cannot take the helm from them and control their course and neither should we expect to do so.

We believe that our gender and our sexuality do not define us

All of us are who we are, not because we are male or female, gay or straight or anything in between – these are just potentially flexible parts of our entirety. Equally so, children are human beings who do not deserve to be straitjacketed by these aspects but need opportunities and freedom to discover and express their human identity. To serve them better, we would therefore do well to:

1. Reflect on our own gender and sexuality

We need to understand ourselves better. How has your gender shaped you at different times in your life? And how important is it? How has your sexuality manifested itself at different stages? How influential are both of these aspects when you describe yourself as a person and when you meet new people?

2. Think about what we ourselves role-model to children

Are you aware of stereotypical thoughts and behaviours in yourself (for they surely exist!)? What verbal and behavioural messages do you give out – consciously or otherwise? What are your emotional reactions and responses to girls and/or boys and their playing behaviours? What do you get fired up or anxious about and why? In what ways do you counteract and/or reinforce stereotypical language and actions? What roles do you take on and why? What might children be learning from you without you realizing it?

3. Try to see the world through children's eyes

Adults have done a whole lot more living than the children in their lives and their brains have less plasticity, so they see things differently to children; although all of us are still in process – we still have much to learn and explore in our adult, early middle and old age. We are not always right and we cannot necessarily or automatically know and understand children and their experiences. Children are living in a different time to us and their world is a very different place to ours – making sense of it is a complex process, and the more so when you consider that children frequently 'read and listen' to behaviour rather than words and our non-verbal communication is often at odds with what we say. We tend to either assume children can understand our instructions very well (and so are being awkward when they appear blank) or we presume they are unable to comprehend all kinds of concepts and information so over protect them (when they may be far more capable and intuitive than we think). Attempting to put ourselves in their position and see things from their changing perspectives is definitely a skill to cultivate, although one not easily mastered. They cannot see the world through an adult lens, but we can strive to see the world a little more as they do – and what an amazing, perplexing and diverse a place it seems to be.

4. Unobtrusively observe and listen to children playing

Many adults have almost certainly lost touch with play which is the lifeblood of children's time and energy. Taking the time to eavesdrop and sensitively watch children playing can yield a whole host of insights and we can learn much about children themselves and about a whole world of play. Developing a curiosity about and a healthy respect for play will yield a ripe harvest of alternative perspectives and reawaken the child in us with a whole new world of possibilities. It should also help us interrupt and interfere less in children's play and respect that this is their domain.

5. Think about the provision of resources, creation of space and opportunities for play

Children need time and space to play and we should pay attention to the nature of the spaces and the things they can play with to ensure that they have as much variety as possible, and are far less limited or restricted by physical or attitudinal boundaries. Although indoor spaces can be exciting places to play, we all know that it is good for children to be given as much time as is viable in a range of outdoor places, but unfortunately their time and freedom to roam in such spaces has dramatically decreased in recent decades. It takes time, thought and effort on our part to give children non-gender prescriptive loose parts to play with; to lessen the number of obviously gendered toys and books that they have; to increase those that are non-stereotypical and to ensure that we give all boys and girls a wide range of opportunities that are challenging and stimulating. Offering children a rich and diverse play diet is perhaps one of the greatest and most inspired gifts we can offer, because through their playing this gives them the freedom to genuinely experiment and explore their own gender and sexuality and what this means to them.

6. Believe and trust in children's agency, their competence and capability

Whether they are girls or boys, children are not weak, vulnerable and passive and neither are they out of control and needing to be 'tamed', although these opposing attitudes are both common in our society. They are younger human beings with a great deal to offer and teach us. We agree wholeheartedly with Dahlberg (1997: 22) that a child is:

> an active and creative actor, a subject and citizen with potentials, rights and responsibility [...] worth listening to and having a dialogue with and who has the courage to think and act by him or herself – a constructor in the construction of his or her own knowledge and his or her fellow human being's common culture.

Seeing children as competent and capable – even potentially – is a whole new mind-set for many of us, but a vibrant and liberating one for both adults and children alike.

Of course we have no proof that improving and increasing children's play diet makes them happier and more independent in the present (although we have a large number of anecdotes and observations from both adults and children that it does), or that it will make them happier and more rounded individuals in the future (some very complex longitudinal studies would have to be devised to even attempt to prove that). But thoughtlessly encouraging stereotypically gendered play is an unnecessary and limiting constriction. Having a zero tolerance attitude to children exploring sex and sexuality through play is equally constricting and drives it underground. Play is like opening doors for children – whole worlds of possibility for them to explore and when we meddle too much or try to control their playing, it's like telling them to go and play on the beach but to keep their socks and shoes on and not to go in the water. Let's not do that, but respect the power of play as an evolutionary force in their lives.

While researching for and writing this book, we have also learnt a number of things in the process and in the spirit of shared reflective practice, we pass them on here:

- We have learnt to question research – in our opinion all research is biased in some way and has an underlying agenda and few researchers are as objective as they claim to be. This does not invalidate all research claims, but reading others' research with both scepticism and genuine enquiry is a healthy combination.

- Earlier on in our research, we believed that there were probably significant innate differences between girls and boys. At present, we are no longer sure about this but we do think that there are probably a few hard-wired differences, which may have little or less significance than we previously thought, when we consider that the plasticity of the brain continues throughout life and changes and adapts according to experience. Even here though, we think there is still much to learn. Recent research studies seem to be indicating that male and female bodies experience certain illnesses in different ways and respond differently to particular drugs – scientists think that in the future there will be gender specific drugs that will work for one sex and not the other. So, the dance goes on!

- We have been surprised at the number of people we have talked with and interviewed who have fixed views, and who don't question where these came from and very often don't want to change their minds.

- The more we read and ponder about gender, the more we have come to see how it affects us – all of us – very deeply. As Lippa says, 'gender stereotypes are probably the most overlearned and entrenched stereotypes we possess.' (2005: 180)

- We have been struck by how prudish our western attitudes are and how sex is treated as a separate part of life that is imbued with sanctity and hushed up with propriety, especially where children are concerned. In some of our workshops, we asked participants to list all the words that were used in their families to denote penis and vagina and ended up with an astonishing (and often hilarious) array of terms. But it would never cross our minds to teach children to use different words for other non-sexual parts of the body (can you imagine intestines being referred to as 'coily-woilies' or ears being little 'luggies' in case mentioning the real words might in some way be deemed inappropriate?!). We are still deeply affected and unwittingly motivated by centuries of religious and cultural influences and we continue to realize how all pervading this is in Western society.

● Most of all we have learnt that we truly do not see things as they are, but as *we* are.

The subjects of gender, sexuality and play and how we all practice and perform these are pivotal to how we live and are critical to many public policy decisions in education, the military, the workplace, the home, the family, sport and leisure, childcare, the law; each of these and more, elicit complex and unresolved questions about equality and inequality and how these are manifested and practised in our society. It is beyond the scope of this book to list and explore such questions here (although some are posed in Appendix C), but certainly further research in a range of fields is going to be needed for a long time to come, in order for us all to make sense of these issues. But we are left wondering whether better opportunities and freedom to play may have a valid ongoing contribution in addressing the inequalities experienced by today's children who will become tomorrows' adults.

So, this is not the end of this book for us: we will no doubt continue to ponder and occasionally wrestle with it all for the rest of our lives. And we hope it is not the end of the book for you either and that we have inspired and/or provoked you too. We look forward to better comprehending gender, sexuality and play.

APPENDIX A

Playwork Principles

These Principles establish the professional and ethical framework for playwork and as such must be regarded as a whole.

They describe what is unique about play and playwork, and provide the playwork perspective for working with children and young people.

They are based on the recognition that children and young people's capacity for positive development will be enhanced if given access to the broadest range of environments and play opportunities.

1   All children and young people need to play. The impulse to play is innate. Play is a biological, psychological and social necessity, and is fundamental to the healthy development and well being of individuals and communities.

2   Play is a process that is freely chosen, personally directed and intrinsically motivated. That is, children and young people determine and control the content and intent of their play, by following their own instincts, ideas and interests, in their own way for their own reasons.

3   The prime focus and essence of playwork is to support and facilitate the play process and this should inform the development of play policy, strategy, training and education.

4   For playworkers, the play process takes precedence and playworkers act as advocates for play when engaging with adult led agendas.

5   The role of the playworker is to support all children and young people in the creation of a space in which they can play.

6   The playworker's response to children and young people playing is based on a sound up-to-date knowledge of the play process, and reflective practice.

7   Playworkers recognize their own impact on the play space and also the impact of children and young people's play on the playworker.

8 Playworkers choose an intervention style that enables children and
young people to extend their play. All playworker intervention
must balance risk with the developmental benefit and well-being of
children.

(Playwork Principles Scrutiny Group, 2005)

APPENDIX B

Play types

Symbolic play

Play which allows control, gradual exploration and increased under-standing without being out of one's depth, by using symbols, ie. objects, designs or signs to represent people, ideas or qualities. For example, using a piece of wood to symbolize a person or a weapon, a piece of string to symbolize a wedding ring, a length of rope to symbolize a boundary, a carrot to symbolize a microphone; building a shrine, creating a flag.

Exploratory play (or finding out play)

Play to access factual information about an environment and engaging with the area or thing and, either by manipulation or movement, assessing its properties, possibilities and content. For example, stacking bricks, taking a camera apart, digging 'to Australia'.

Object play (or problem-solving play)

Play which uses infinite and interesting sequences of hand-eye manipu-lations and movements. For example, examination and novel use of any object, e.g. cloth, rope, bubblewrap, paintbrush, cup. The fascination here is with the object itself and what it can do or be (regardless of what it's 'proper use' might be).

Rough and tumble play

Close encounter play which is less to do with fighting and more to do with touching, tickling, gauging relative strength, discovering physical flexibility and the exhilaration of display. Finding out and testing one's own and other's limits. Learning social and interpersonal codes of physical conduct. For example, playful fighting, wrestling and chasing during which the children are obviously unhurt and give every indication that they are enjoying themselves.

Socio-dramatic play

The enactment of real and potential experiences of an intense personal, social, domestic or interpersonal nature, i.e. recreating scenes from own life. For example, playing at house, going to the shops, being mums and dads, organizing a meal, having a row, attending funerals, presiding over divorce courts. Sometimes acting out emotions too scary to express in real life – often therapeutic.

Dramatic play

Play which dramatizes events in which the child is not a direct participator, i.e. recreating scenes from others' lives or from telly or theatre. For example, representation of a TV show, an event on the street or in the news, a religious or festive event, a birth or death or being famous footballers or a band in a recent match or concert. Sometimes done for an audience.

Social play

Play during which the rules and criteria for social engagement, interaction and communication can be revealed, explored and amended. Any social or interactive situation which contains an expectation on all parties that they will discuss and abide by certain rules, customs or protocols, e.g. games, conversations, making something together, challenging, discussing, and so on.

Communication play

Play using words, nuances or gestures, for example, mime, jokes, play acting, mickey taking, singing, debate, poetry, graffiti, swearing, making up languages/words/slang, storytelling. Creating a reaction and exploring the impact.

Creative play (inventive play)

Play which allows a new response, an expression of self, the transformation of information, awareness of new connections and new insights, with an element of surprise. It is about focused, but spontaneous creation with a wide range of materials and tools for its own sake, with real freedom and not necessarily an end result. Could be small or large scale, individual or group.

Deep play

Play which allows the child to encounter risky or even potentially life threatening experiences, to develop survival skills and conquer fear. For example, leaping onto an aerial runway, riding a bike on a parapet, balancing on a high beam. The risk will be from the child's perspective (certainly not the adults') and so the same experience could be deep play for one child and not the next.

Fantasy play

Play which rearranges the world in the child's way, a way which is complete fantasy and unreal, e.g. being superheroes, aliens, goblins, time lords, flying a UFO, casting spells, saving the world from certain destruction, and so on.

Imaginative play

Play where the conventional rules that govern the physical world do not apply, but is still based on reality. For example, imagining you are, or pretending to be, a tree, a ship, or an animal, patting a dog which isn't there, having an invisible friend, imagining a table is a bus or a cave, and so on.

Role play

Play exploring identity and ways of being and doing, although not normally of an intense personal, social, domestic or interpersonal nature. Often imitating someone or trying out something seen but not experienced, e.g. driving a car, playing dead, being a clown or a shopkeeper.

Locomotor play

Movement in any and every direction – up down, along, at various speeds and seemingly for its own sake. For example, chase, tag, hide and seek, tree climbing, rolling, jumping, dancing. Experiencing the possibilities of one's body within a particular environment. Includes ranging.

Mastery play

Generally expressed by taking (and feeling) control of the physical and affective ingredients of the natural environment. For example, digging holes and tunnels in earth or sand, changing the course of streams, constructing shelters, building fires. However, could also include mastering a new skill, e.g. a jump across a river, or riding a bike.

Recapitulative play

Play that displays aspects of human evolutionary history, stored and passed on through our genes and manifested when children play spontaneously – often stimulated by aspects of the outdoor environment like forests and shallow pools/rivers. For example, Lighting fires, engaging in spontaneous rituals and songs, dressing up in historic clothes/uniforms and role-playing, playing wars and making weapons, growing and cooking things, creating ancient style communities, building shelters, creating languages and religions.

(Adapted from Hughes, B. (2002) *A Taxonomy Of Play Types*, 2nd edn, London: Playlink. Used by permission.)

APPENDIX C

The subjects of gender and sexuality and play and how we all practice and perform these are pivotal to how we live and critical to many public policy decisions in different fields. The following are examples of some of the numerous complex and unresolved questions that we could be asking. While many of them may need rephrasing and/or recontextualizing, they are all relevant to how gender, sexuality and play are perceived and manifested in the present day and may well be questions worthy of further research.

Education

- Is it better or worse to teach boys and girls separately?
- Should boys start school later than girls?
- Should there be more men working in nurseries and primary schools?
- Should sex education be an implicit and ongoing part of the whole curriculum?
- Should sex education cover sexual pleasure as well as sexual health and reproduction?
- Should all teachers undergo training in gender and sexuality issues?
- Should we encourage more girls into science and engineering careers and more boys into caring professions? And, if so, why and how?
- Should we encourage more boys into creative careers such as hairdressing, beauty, clothes design and so on? And, if so, why and how?
- Why is there a 'digital divide' in how boys and girls adjust to and use computers?

The workplace

- Should men and women be always paid equally for equal work?
- Should we treat working mothers differently to working fathers with regard to childcare and paternity/maternity leave and benefits?
- Are expectations of overtime, long hours and competitive initiative fair? Or do they favour childless employees or absent fathers?
- Should we prioritize more affordable high-quality childcare?
- Why are women still so under-represented in boardrooms?
- Do women and men have different styles of leadership?
- How should we respond to sexual harassment?

The military

- Should men and women have equal or different roles?
- Should more women enter the forces – at all levels?
- Should women also be on the frontline in combat?

Home and family

- Are women better or different caretakers to men or do they both have the same potential?
- Do women and men parent differently? Are single parent families, gay/lesbian parent families really any different?
- Should there be a difference in the division of labour? Why are some tasks deemed more male than female and vice-versa?
- Should we think more broadly about who has custody of children and who can foster children?
- What are the roots of domestic violence? Can we change them? How?
- Is sexual violence primarily a male problem? And, if so, why?
- Why do so many couples separate and seem unable to work out their differences?

Sport and leisure

● Should all sportsmen and sportswomen be paid or rewarded on equal terms for participating in the same sports?

● Should all popular sports be given the same status nationally and in the media regardless of whether they are played mainly by men, by women or by both?

● Should traditionally male and female arts and sports be compulsory at school for both sexes? And should they be equally marketed to adult men and women?

The law

● Should men and women receive the same sentences for the same crimes?

● Should hormones be considered in relation to violent offences carried out by either men or women?

● Should there be equal numbers of male and female jurors at each trial?

● Should there be equal numbers of male and female judges, politicians and anybody who in some way affects the law?

Play

● Should schools have a play-based curriculum up to the age of seven?

● Do children learn more, academically, if they have outdoor classrooms?

● Do children learn more, academically, if they have freely chosen play outdoors at lunchtime?

● Should playwork be given the same status as early years and youth work?

● Should we have a national play strategy that recognizes Article 31 of the UNCRC (United Nations Charter on the Rights of the Child) and which includes a statutory duty on local authorities (including

Public Health) to plan and budget for area wide public play provision and playable public space?

● Should the training for all adult professionals who come into contact with children include an understanding of the benefits of free play? (For example, doctors, coaches, teachers, social workers etc.)

● Should the training of all adult professionals whose work indirectly affects children include an understanding of play and how their work impacts on children's play? (For example, town planners, police, landscape architects, etc.)

GLOSSARY

Adulteration Describes the intervention of an adult that effectively stops, changes or tries to control children's play. Such intervention usually does not recognize children's own competence or capability or attempt to consider what might really be happening. It can happen for a number of reasons such as health and safety, education and behaviour management that appear justifiable at the time, but often arise from the adult feeling anxious, angry, concerned, superior or even playful.

Adventure playground An adventure playground is not the fixed wooden play area that seems to be in popular usage. Based on their evolution from European children playing on waste land and old bomb sites several decades ago, they describe now a space dedicated solely to children's play, where skilled playworkers enable and facilitate the ownership, development and design of that space – physically, socially and culturally – by the children playing there. Activities not normally condoned in other spaces where children play – such as digging, making fires or building and demolishing dens are provided for and encouraged. (Adapted from *Play England's Practice Briefing No.1 – the Essential Elements of an AdventurePplayground.*)

Article 31 One of the articles in the United Nations Convention on the Rights of the Child, which recognizes the right of every child to rest, leisure, play, recreational activities and free and full participation in cultural and artistic life. Essentially, in upholding children's rights to play, this article upholds their right to *be* children in the here and now.

Borderwork Actions and activities that children engage in that can both strengthen the gender divide and/or chart their attempts to cross implicitly recognized gender boundaries.

Causal cascades A series of influences that merge to create a whole system that is greater than the sum of its parts e.g. biological and genetic factors; family, peer, social and cultural influences; thoughts and cognition; emotions, feelings and attitudes and behaviour all influence the expression of gender – causal cascades that affect gender (after Maccoby 1998).

Causal thickets Hard to analyse tangles of influence (as above) that interact via many interlocking feedback loops.

Children's agency Describing children's active operation with the world around them including concepts and ideas as well as people, things and environments.

Femininity Portraying those qualities popularly associated with women.

Feminism   The advocacy of women's rights on the grounds of the equality of the sexes.

Gender norms   Expectations shared by a group, at a given point in time, that reflect a commonly accepted set of activities and ways of presenting oneself as either a man or a woman.

Genderscape   A whole physical, social and psychological environment that has been influenced by cultural gender expectations.

Heteronormativity   The unquestioned expectation that all children are/will be heterosexual – expressed often unconsciously through adults' words and behaviours and through books, activities and the media.

Intersex   The term given to describe people who are born with ambiguous genitalia or who are discovered to have chromosomal or hormonal conditions or physical attributes that would not be described as 'wholly male' or 'wholly female'.

LGBT   An initialism that stands for lesbian, gay, bisexual, and transgender.

Loose parts   A term first coined by landscape architect Nicholson to describe materials with varied properties that can be moved and manipulated in many ways by the player(s). Nicholson purported 'In any environment, both the degree of inventiveness and creativity and the possibility of discovery are directly proportional to the number and kind of variables in it' (1971) and advocated for a huge range of both synthetic and natural non-prescriptive materials to be made available to playing children.

Masculinity   Portraying those qualities popularly associated with men.

Nature/nurture debate   Long-running discussion about gender being caused either by biological or psychological and sociological influences.

Play culture   The way in which children cultivate themselves and their surroundings – dependent on their participation and activity in informal social networks thus enabling traditional transmission of the culture from child to child.

Play deprivation   The notion that the absence of play opportunities are likely to deprive children of experiences that are regarded as developmentally essential and result in those affected being both biologically and socially disabled. Such disablement would be on a spectrum of disadvantage related to the levels and kinds of deprivation.

Play menu   Sometimes also known as the 'playwork curriculum', this sets out a framework for consistently creating and resourcing a play environment that offers and supports a wide range of essential play experiences. It can be used as an audit tool for individual or peer reflection that fully explores and maximizes not just the properties of the physical environment but also the human environment – the attitudes and behaviours of the adults and children present and how these can best support children's freedom, independence and self-expression.

Play types   Based on a research and literature review and observations of children playing, these represent Bob Hughes' classification of sixteen different ways of playing that children naturally engage in both physically and emotionally (see Appendix 2). They describe what we might see and hear in each case and the possible purposes of such playing.

Playwork   A low-intervention

approach that supports children's self-directed free play by creating rich play environments and sourcing non-prescriptive materials for children to use as they wish. Whilst anyone working with children can learn to use this approach, professional playworkers additionally work to support children playing through unobtrusive observation and reflection on personal reactions and adult agendas, in order to only sensitively intervene when absolutely necessary, thereby ensuring that the control of play remains with children themselves.

Playwork principles These Principles establish the professional and ethical framework for playwork by describing what is unique about play and playwork and providing the playwork perspective for working with children and young people. They are based on the recognition that children and young people's capacity for positive development will be enhanced if given access to the broadest range of environments and play opportunities.

Scrapstore playpods Wooden or metal structures filled with clean and safe waste such as tyres, cardboard, tubing, material, clothes, bags, rope, boxes, foam etc. for children to play with. Scrapstore playpods are constructed in primary school playgrounds as part of a training, mentoring and support consultancy package with the whole school community to transform play at lunchtimes. See www.playpods.co.uk.

Stereotype This word originally described a printing plate cast from a mould of composed type. In popular use today as both a noun and a verb, it refers to the judgement made about a person or thing that conforms to an unjustifiably fixed mental picture.

REFERENCES

Abrams, R. (1997), *The Playful Self*, London: Fourth Estate.

Ackerley, J. (2003), 'Gender Differences in the Folklore Play Of Children in Primary School Playgrounds', *Play and Folklore* (44): 2–15.

Anggard, E. (2011), 'Children's Gendered and Non-Gendered Play in Natural Spaces', *Children, Youth and Environments* 21 (2): 5–33. Available online: http://www.colorado.edu/journals/cye (accessed 12 August 2014).

Aydt, H. and W. Corsaro (2003), 'Differences in Children's Construction of Gender across Culture: An Interpretive Approach', *Behavioural Scientist* (46): 1306, Available online: http://abs.sagepub.com/cgi/content/abstract/46/10/1306 (accessed on 5 June 2015).

Bailey, R. (2002) 'Playing Social Chess: Children's Play and Social Intelligence', *Early Years* 22 (2): 163–73.

Bailey, R. (2011), *Letting Children Be Children* (Report of an Independent Review of the Commercialisation & Sexualisation of Childhood), Department for Education.

Bancroft, J. (ed.) (2003), *Sexual Development in Childhood*, Bloomington: Indiana University Press.

Barford, V. (2014), 'Do Children's Toys Influence Their Career Choices?', *BBC News Magazine* (January). Available online: http://www.bbc.co.uk/news/magazine-25857895 (accessed on 2 June 2015).

Baron-Cohen, S. (2004), *Essential Difference: Male and Female Brains and the Truth about Autism*, New York: Basic Books.

Bateson, G. (1955), A *Theory of Play and Fantasy, Approaches to the Study of Human Personality: American Psychiatric Association Psychiatric Research Reports* 2: 39–51. Cited in Andresen (2005) 'Role Play and Language Development in the Preschool Years', *Culture and Psychology* 11 (4): 387–414.

Bateson, P. and P. Martin (2013), *Play, Playfulness, Creativity and Innovation*, Cambridge: Cambridge University Press.

Bead, Carol R. (1994), *The Development of Gender Roles*, New York: McGraw-Hill Inc.

Becker, J. B., K. J. Berkley, N. Geary, E. Hampson, J. P. Herman and E. A. Young, (eds), (2008), *Sex Differences in the Brain from Genes to Behaviour*, New York: Oxford University Press.

Bekoff, M. (2007), *The Emotional Lives of Animals*, California: New World Library.

Bekoff, M. and Byers, J. A. eds. (1998), *Animal Play*, Cambridge University Press.

Bem, S. Lipsitz (1983), 'Gender Schema Theory and its Implications for Child Development: Raising Gender-Aschematic Children in a Gender-Schematic Society', *Signs: Journal of Women in Culture and Society* (8): 598–616.

Bem, S. Lipsitz (1998), *An Unconventional Family*, New Haven, CT: Yale University Press.

Berenbaum S. A. and Hines, M. (1992), 'Early Androgens are related to Childhood Sex-typed Toy Preferences', *Psychological Science* 3 (3): 203–6.

Berenbaum, S., C. Martin, L. Hanish, P. Briggs and R. Fobes (2008), 'Sex Differences in Children's Play', in J. Becker, J. Berkley, N. Geary, E. Hampson, J. P. Herman and E. A. Young (eds), *Sex Differences in the Brain from Genes to Behaviour*, 275–90, New York: Oxford University Press.

Beunderman, J. (2010), *People Make Play*, London: NCB.

Biddulph, S. (1998), *Raising Boys*, London: HarperCollins.

Biddulph, S. (2013), *Raising Girls*, London: Harper Thorsons.

Bjorkland, D. (2007), *Why Youth Is Not Wasted on the Young: Immaturity in Human Development*, Oxford: Blackwell Publishing.

Blatchford, P., E. Baines and A. Pellegrini (2003), 'The Social Context of School Playground Games: Sex and Ethnic Differences, and Changes Over Time After Entry To Junior School', *British Journal of Developmental Psychology* 21: 481–505.

Brennan, H. and J. Graham (2012), 'Is This Normal? Understanding Your Child's Sexual Behaviour'. FPQ Family Planning Queensland. Available online: http://www.fpq.com.au/publications/teachingAids/Is_this_normal.php (accessed 6 June 2015).

Brizendine, L. (2007), *The Female Brain*, London: Bantam Press.

Brizendine, L. (2010), *The Male Brain*, New York: Broadway Books.

Broadwell, M. M. (1969), 'Teaching For Learning', *The Gospel Guardian* 20 (41): 1–3.

Brooker, L. (2006), 'From Home to Home Corner: Observing Children's Identity Maintenance in Early Childhood Settings' *Children and Society* 20 (2): 16–127.

Brown, C. S. (2014), *Parenting Beyond Pink and Blue: How To Raise Your Kids Free of Gender Stereotypes*, New York: Ten Speed Press.

Brown, F. (2014), *Play & Playwork: 101 Stories of Children Playing*, Maidenhead: Open University Press.

Brown, S. (2009), *Play – How It Shapes the Brain, Opens the Imagination and Invigorates the Soul*, London: Avery.

Brown, S. L. (1998), 'Play As An Organising Principle: Clinical Evidence And Personal Observations', in M. Bekoff and J. Byers (eds), *Animal Play: Comparative and Ecological Perspectives*, Cambridge: Cambridge University Press. Available online: http://hwww.exuberantanimal.com/web/library/case_for_the_body_resources/play/stuart_play_as_organizing_prin.pdf (accessed 19 May 2015).

Brown, S. L. and J. Lomax (1969), 'A Pilot Study of Young Murderers', the Hogg Foundation Annual Report, Texas, in B. Hughes, *Evolutionary Playwork*, 2nd edn, 192, New York: Routledge.

Bruner, J. S. (1972), 'Nature and Uses of Immaturity', *American Psychologist* 27 (8): 28–60.

Bruner, J. S. (1983), 'Play, Thought, and Language', *Peabody Journal of Education* 60 (3): 60–9.

Buckingham, D., R. Willett, S. Bragg and R. Russell (2010), *Sexualised Goods Aimed At Children*, Report to the Scottish Parliament Equal Opportunities

Committee, Scottish Parliament Equal Opportunities Committee, Edinburgh, UK.

Burghardt, G. M. (2005), *The Genesis of Animal Play*, Cambridge, MA: MIT Press.

Burke, P. (1996), *Gender Shock*, New York: Anchor Books.

Butler, J. (1990), *Gender Trouble: Feminism and the Subversion of Identity*, New York: Routledge.

Byron, T. (2008), *Safer Children in a Digital World*, Report of the Byron Review, London: DCSF Publications.

Caillois, R. (2001), *Man, Play and Games*, Champaign, IL: Illinois University Press.

Cavanagh-Johnson, T. (1991), 'Understanding The Sexual Behaviours Of Young Children', *SIECUS Report* August/September. Available online: www.siecus.org/_data/global/images/SIECUS%20Report%202/19-6.pdf (accessed 3 February 2015).

Cavanagh-Johnson, T. (2013), *Understanding Children's Sexual Behaviours – What's Natural and Healthy*, San Diego, CA: Institute on Violence, Abuse and Trauma.

Cealy–Harrison, W. and J. Hood–Williams (2002), *Beyond Sex and Gender*, London: Sage Publications Ltd.

Chown, A. (2014), *Play Therapy in the Outdoors*, London: Jessica Kingsley Publishers.

Cobb, E. (1977), *The Ecology of Imagination in Childhood*, New York: Columbia University Press.

Cole-Hamilton, I., A. Harrop and C. Street (2002), *Making the Case for Play*, London: National Children's Bureau.

Cranny-Francis, A., W. Waring, P. Stavropoulos and J. Kirby (2002), *Gender Studies: Terms and Debates*, Basingstoke: Palgrave MacMillan.

Cranwell, K. (1999), 'Children's Street Play and Games 1880–1920', in B. Hughes (ed.), *The Proceedings of the 14th Annual Play and Human Development Meeting (Part 2)*, Ely, Cambridgeshire: Playeducation.

Crowe, B. (1983), *Play Is A Feeling*, London: George Allen & Unwin.

Cunningham, H. (2006), *The Invention of Childhood*, London: BBC Books.

Dahlberg, G. (1997), 'The Child and the Pedagogue as Co-constructors of Culture and Knowledge', in *Voices about Swedish Childcare*, SoS Report, Stockholm: Socialstyrelsen.

Davies, B. (1989), *Frogs And Snails And Feminist Tale: Pre-School Children And Gender*, Sydney, Australia: Allen and Unwin.

Davies, B. (1997), 'The Construction of Gendered Identities Through Play', in B. Davies and D. Corson (eds), *Encyclopaedia of Language and Education Volume 3; Oral Discourse and Education*, Norwell, MA: Kluwer Academic Publisher. Available online: http://link.springer.com/chapter/10.1007%2F978-94-011-4417-9_12 (accessed 6 June 2015).

Davin, A. (1995), *Growing Up Poor: Home, School And Street In London, 1817–1940*, London: Rivers Oram Press.

Doidge, N. (2014), 'Sex on the Brain – What Brain Plasticity Teaches About Internet Porn', *Hungarian Review* 4 (3044). Available online: http://www.yourbrainonporn.com/sex-brain-what-brain-plasticity-teaches-about-internet-porn-2014-norman-doidge-md (accessed 2 February 2015).

Drach, K. M, J. Wientzen and L. R. Ricci (2001), 'The Diagnostic Utility Of Sexual Behavior Problems In Diagnosing Sexual Abuse In A Forensic Child Abuse Evaluation Clinic', *Child Abuse and Neglect* (4): 489–503.

Eckert, P. and S. McConnell-Ginet (2003), *Language and Gender*, 2nd edn, Cambridge: Cambridge University Press. Available online: http://web.stanford. edu/~eckert/PDF/Chap1.pdf (accessed 6 June 2015).

Egan, R. D. and G. L. Hawkes (2008), 'Imperilled And Perilous: Exploring The History Of Childhood Sexuality', *Journal of Historical Sociology* 21 (4): 355–67.

Eliot, L. (2010), *Pink Brain Blue Brain*, Oxford: One World Publications.

Elkind, D. (2007), *The Power of Play*, Philadelphia: Da Capo Press.

Ellis, L., S. Hershberger, E. Field, S. Wersinger, S. Pellis, D. Geary, C. Palmer, K., Hoyenga, A. Hetsroni and K. Karadi (2008), *Sex Differences: Summarizing More Than a Century of Scientific Research*, New York: Psychology Press.

Ellis, M. J. (1973), *Why People Play*, Upper Saddle River, NJ: Prentice-Hall.

Else, P. (2014), *Making Sense of Play*, Maidenhead: Open University Press.

Erikson, E. H. (1965), *Childhood and Society*, New York: Norton & Co.

Erikson, E. H. (1977), *Toys and Reasons*, New York: Norton & Co.

Evaldsson, A. C. (2003), 'Throwing Like a Girl? Situating Gender Differences in Physicality Across Game Contexts', *Childhood* 10 (4): 475–97.

Fagen, R. M. (1981), *Animal Play Behaviour*, Oxford: Oxford University Press.

Fausto-Sterling, A. (2000), *Sexing the Body: Gender Politics and the Construction of Sexuality*, New York: Basic Books.

Fine, C. (2011), *Delusions of Gender*, London: Icon Books.

Frayser, S. G. (1994), 'Defining Normal Childhood Sexuality: An Anthropological Approach', *Annual Review of Sex Research* (5): 173–217.

Frayser, S. G. (2003), 'Cultural Dimensions of Childhood Sexuality in the United States', in J. Bancroft (ed.), *Sexual Development in Childhood*, Bloomington, IN: Indiana University Press.

Friedrich, W. N. (2003), 'Studies of Sexuality of Non-abused Children', in J. Bancroft (ed.), *Sexual Development in Childhood*, Bloomington, IN: Indiana University Press.

Friedrich, W. N., J. Fisher, D. Broughton, M. Houston and C. R. Shafran (1998), 'Normative Sexual Behaviour in Children: A Contemporary Sample', *Pediatrics* 101 (4).

Gagnon, J. and W. Simon (1973), *Sexual Conduct – the Social Sources of Human Sexuality*, Chicago, IL: Aldine Publishing.

Garvey, C. (1977), *Play*, London: Fontana/Open Books Publishing.

Gaskins, S., W. Haight, and D. F. Lancy (2007), 'The Cultural Construction of Play', in Gayle Rubin, 'The Traffic in Women', *Toward an Anthropology of Women*, New York: Monthly Review Press.

Gayler, K. and I. Evans (2001), *Pretend Play and the Development of Emotion Regulation in Preschool Children, Early Child Development and Care*, Vol. 166 Issue 6, Taylor and Francis online (accessed 26 April 2016).

Gibson, C. L. (2013), 'Cerebral Ischemic Stroke – is Gender Important?,' *Journal of Cerebral Blood Flow & Metabolism* 33: 1355–61.

Goldberg, S (2004), *The Inevitability of Patriarchy*, New York: William Morrow and Company.

Goodall, J. (1990), *Through a Window: 30 Years Observing the Gombe Chimpanzees*, London: Weidenfeld & Nicolson.

Goodwin, M. H. (2001), 'Organizing Participation in Cross-Sex Jump Rope: Situating Gender Differences within Longitudinal Studies of Activities', *Research on Language and Social Interaction* 34 (1): 75–106. Available online: http://dx.doi.org/10.1207/S15327973RLSI3401_4 (accessed 2 June 2016).

Goodwin, M. H. (2006), *The Hidden Life of Girls*, Oxford: Blackwell.

Gray, P. (2013), *Free to Learn*, New York: Basic Books.

Green, R. (1987), *The 'Sissy Boy Syndrome' and the Development of Homosexuality*, New Haven, CT: Yale University Press.

Groos, K., (1901), *The Play of Man*, trans. Elizabeth L. Baldwin. New York: Appleton.

Gurian, M. (2011), *Boys & Girls Learn Differently*, San Francisco, CA: Jossey-Bass.

Harris, M. (1977), *Cannibals and Kings: Origins of Cultures*, New York: Random House.

Harris, R. H. (1994), *Let's Talk about Sex*, London: Walker Books.

Hart, R. (1997), *Children's Participation, the Theory and Practice of Involving Young Citizens in Community Development and Environmental Care*, London: Earthscan Publications Ltd.

Hines, M. (2004), *Brain Gender*, Oxford: Oxford University Press.

Holland, P. (2003/08), *We Don't Play with Guns Here: War, Weapon and Superhero Play in the Early Years*, Maidenhead: Open University Press.

Hughes, B. (1996), *Play Environments: A Question of Quality*, London: Playlink.

Hughes, B. (2001), *Evolutionary Playwork and Reflective Analytic Practice*, London: Routledge.

Hughes, B. (2002), *The First Claim – Desirable Processes*, Cardiff: Play Wales.

Hughes, B. (2012), *Evolutionary Playwork*, 2nd edn, London: Routledge.

Huizinga, J. (1955), *Homo Ludens*, London: Beacon.

Huxley, A. (1932/2007), *Brave New World*, Vintage Classics.

Hyde, J. S. (2005), 'The Gender Similarities Hypothesis', *American Psychologist* 60: 581–92.

Jackson, S. (1982), *Childhood Sexuality*, Oxford: Blackwell.

Jenkins, P. (1998), *Moral Panic*, New Haven, CT: Yale University Press.

Jenkins, S. (2014), 'Our Addiction to Criminalizing Human Behaviour Makes a Mockery of Private Responsibility', *The Guardian*, 6 November. Available online: http://www.theguardian.com/commentisfree/2014/nov/06/addiction-criminalising-behaviour-private-responsibility (accessed 20 October 2015).

Jenkinson, S. (2001), *The Genius of Play*, Stroud: Hawthorne.

Johnston, J. E., (2011), 'Children Who are Cruel to Animals: When to Worry', *Psychology Today*, 27 April. Available online: https://www.psychologytoday.com/blog/the-human-equation/201104/children-who-are-cruel-animals-when-worry (accessed 4 June 2015).

Jones, P. (2009), *Rethinking Childhood: Attitudes in Contemporary Society*, London: Continuum.

Jordan-Young, R. M. (2011), *Brainstorm – The Flaws in the Science of Sex Differences*, Cambridge, MA: Harvard University Press.

Kalliala, M. (2006), *Play Culture in a Changing World*, Maidenhead, Berkshire: Open University Press.

Kane, E. (2006) '"No Way My Boys Are Going to be Like That": Parents

Responses to Children's Gender Nonconformity': *Gender and Society* 20 (2): 149–76.

Kane, E. (2009), Interview, in P. Jones, *Rethinking Childhood: Attitudes in Contemporary Society*, Continuum.

Kane, E. W. (2012), *The Gender Trap*, New York: New York University Press.

Kane, E. W. (2013), *Rethinking Gender and Sexuality in Childhood*, London: Bloomsbury.

Karsten, L. (2003), 'Children's Use of Public Space – the Gendered World of the Playground', *Childhood* 10 (4): 457–73.

Katch, J. (2001), *Discovering the Meaning of Children's Violent Play*, Boston, MA: Beacon Press

Kehilly, M. J., Mac An Ghail, D. Epstein and P. Redman (2002), 'Private Girls and Public Worlds: Producing Femininities in the Primary School', *Discourse, Special issue on friendship*, 23(2), pp. 167–78.

Kilvington, J. and A. Wood (2010), *Reflective Playwork*, London: Bloomsbury.

Kilvington, J. and A. Wood (2012), 'Sex Differences, Sexuality and Gender Identity – What's Play Got To Do With It?', paper for International Play Association Conference 2012.

Krafchick, J., T. Simmerman, S. Haddock and J. Banning (2005), 'Best-selling Books Advising Parents About Gender: A Feminist Analysis', *Family Relations* 54: 84–100.

Lamb, S. and M. Coakley (1993), 'Normal Childhood Sexual Play and Games: Differentiating Play from Abuse', *Child Abuse & Neglect* (4): 515–26.

Leaper, D. J. and J. Smith (2004), 'A Meta-Analytic Review of Gender Variations in Children's Talk: Talkativeness, Affiliative Speech and Assertive Speech', *Developmental Psychology* 40: 993–1027.

Leinbach, M. D., Hort, B. and Fagot, B. I. (1993), 'Metaphorical Dimensions and the Gender Typing of Toys'. Paper presented at the Symposium conducted at the meeting of the Society for Research in Child Development, New Orleans, Louisiana.

Lester, S. and W. Russell (2008), *Play for a Change*, London: NCB.

Lester, S. and W. Russell (2010), *Children's Right to Play: An Examination of the Importance of Play in the Lives of Children Worldwide*, Working Paper No. 57. The Hague, The Netherlands: Bernard van Leer Foundation.

Levin, D. E. and J. Kilbourne (2008), *So Sexy, So Soon*, New York: Ballantine Books.

Levine, J. (2002), *Harmful to Minors – The Perils of Protecting Children from Sex*, New York: Thunder's Mouth Press.

Liekens, G. (2015), 'Why Britain Needs To Ramp Up Its Sex Education', *Radio Times*, 6 August. Available online: http://www.radiotimes.com/news/2015-08-06/why-britain-needs-to-ramp-up-its-sex-education (accessed 20 October 2015).

Lillemyr, O. F. (2009), *Taking Play Seriously*, Charlotte, NC: Information Age Publishing.

Lippa, R. A. (2005), *Gender, Nature and Nurture*, New York: Psychology Press.

Luker, K. (2007), *When Sex Goes to School*, New York: Norton & Co.

Lytton, H. and D. M. Romney (1991), 'Parents' Differential Socialization of Boys and Girls: A Meta-Analysis': *Psychological Bulletin* 109: 267–96.

Maccoby, E. E. (2003), *The Two Sexes – Growing Up Apart – Coming Together*, Cambridge, MA: The Belknap Press.

Martin, B. (2011), *Children at Play – Learning Gender in the Early Years*, London: Institute of Education Press.

Martin, K. (2005), 'William Wants a Doll. Can He Have One? Feminists, Childcare Advisors and Gender Neutral Childrearing', *Gender and Society* 19 (4): 456–79.

Martinson, F. M. (1973). *Infant and Child Sexuality: A Sociological Perspective*, Saint Peter, MN: The Book Mark (Gustavas Aldolphus College).

Martinson, F. M. (1994), *The Sexual Life of Children*, Westport, CT: Bergin & Garvey.

Mayall (2002), *Towards a Sociology for Childhood – Thinking from Children's Lives*, Maidenhead: Open University Press.

Mayhew, E., Uprichard, E., Beresford, B., Ridge, T. and Bradshaw, J. (2004) 'Children and Childhood in the United Kingdom' in An-Magritt Jensen, Asher Ben-Arieh, Cinzia Conti, Dagmar Kutsar, Maire Nic Ghiolla Phadraig & Hanne Warming Neilsen (eds), *Children's Welfare in Ageing Europe, Volume 1*. Trondheim: Norway Centre for Child Research.

McMahon, L. (2009), *The Handbook of Play Therapy*, 2nd edn, Hove: Routledge.

Mediterranean Institute of Gender Studies, (2005–9), 'Glossary of Gender Related Terms', J. Christodoulou and A. Zobnina (compilers), Mediterranean Institute of Gender Studies. Available online: http://www.medinstgenderstudies.org/wp-content/uploads/Gender-Glossary-updated_final.pdf (accessed 4 June 2015).

Meire, J. (n.d.), *Qualitative Research on Children's Play: A Review of Recent Literature*, Belgium: Childhood & Society Research Centre. Available online: http://iccp-play.org/documents/brno/meire.pdf (accessed 6 June 2015).

Meyer-Bahlburg (2003), 'General Discussion', in J. Bancroft (ed.), *Sexual Development in Childhood*, Bloomington, IN; Indiana University Press.

Millar, S. (1968), *Psychology of Play*, London: Pelican.

Moir, A. and D. Jessel (1991), *Brain Sex – The Real Difference Between Men & Women*, New York: Delta.

Montgomery, H. (2010), 'Focusing on the Child, Not the Prostitute', *Wagadu: Journal of Transnational Women's & Gender Studies* 8: 166–88.

Morrow, V. (n.d.) 'The Ethics of Social Research with Children and Young People – an Overview', Institute of Education, University of London. Available online: http://www.ciimu.org/webs/wellchi/reports/workshop_1/w1_morrow.pdf (accessed 7 July 2014).

Newman, M., Woodcock, A. and Dunham, P. (2006), 'Playtime in the Borderlands: Children's Representations of School, Gender and Bullying through Photographs and Interviews', *Children's Geographies* 3 (3): 345–62.

Newman, R. (2008), 'It Starts in the Womb: Helping Parents Understand Infant Sexuality', *Electronic Journal of Human Sexuality* 11. Available online: http://www.ejhs.org/volume11/Newman.htm (accessed 2 June 2015).

Newson, J. and E. Newson (1979), *Toys and Playthings*, London: Allen & Unwin.

Nicholson, S. (1971), 'How Not to Cheat Children – the Theory of Loose Parts', *Landscape Architecture* 62 (1): 30–5.

Nin, A. (1961), *Seduction of the Minotaur*, Chicago, IL: The Swallow Press.

Nouwen, H. J. M. (1976), *Reaching Out*, Glasgow: William Collins Sons & Co. Ltd.

O'Sullivan, L. F. (2003), 'Methodological Issues Associated with Studies of Child Sexual Behaviour', in J. Bancroft (ed.), *Sexual Development in Childhood*, Bloomington, IN: Indiana University Press.

Opie, I. and P. Opie (1977), *The Lore and Language of School Children*, St. Albans: Granada Publishing Ltd.

Orenstein, Peggy (2011), 'The Ghettoisation of Pink: How It Has Cornered the Little Girl Market', extract from *Cinderella Ate my Daughter*, *Observer*, 19 June.

Organisation Intersex International Australia (2013), 'On the Number of Intersex People'. Available online: https://oii.org.au/16601/intersex-numbers/ (accessed 25 June 2015).

Ortner, Sherry B. (1974), 'Is Female to Male as Nature is to Culture?', in M. Z. Rosaldo and L. Lamphere (eds), *Woman, Culture, and Society*, Stanford, CA: Stanford University Press.

Padawer, Ruth (2012), 'What's So Bad About a Boy Who Wants To Wear a Dress?', *New York Times*, 8 August. Available online: http://www.nytimes.com/2012/08/12/magazine/whats-so-bad-about-a-boy-who-wants-to-wear-a-dress.html?pagewanted=all&_r=0 (accessed 26 January 2016).

Paley, V. G. (2014), *Boys and Girls: Superheroes in the Doll Corner*, Chicago: University of Chicago Press.

Panksepp, J. (2007), 'Can Play Diminish ADHD and Facilitate the Construction of the Social Brain?', *Journal of the Canadian Academy of Child & Adolescent Psychiatry* 16 (2).

Papadopoulos, L. (2010), *Sexualisation of Young People Review*, Crown Copyright, London, England.

Parsons, J. E. (1983), 'Sexual Socialisation and Gender Roles in Childhood', in E. R. Algier and N. B. McCormick (eds), *Changing Boundaries: Gender Roles and Sexual Behaviour*, Palo Alto, CA: Mayfield.

Pasterski, V. L., Geffner, M. E., Brain, C., Hindmarsh, P., Brook, C. and Hines. M. (2005), 'Prenatal Hormones and Postnatal Socialization by Parents as Determinants of Male-Typical Toy Play in Girls with Congenital Adrenal Hyperplasia', *Child Development* 76 (1): 264–78.

Pellegrini, A. D. (2009), *The Role of Play in Human Development*, Oxford: Oxford University Press.

Pellegrini, A. D., P. Blatchford, K. Kato and E. Baines (2004), 'A Short-Term Longitudinal Study of Children's Playground Games in Primary School: Implications for Adjustment to School and Social Adjustment in the USA and the UK', *Social Development* 13: 107–23.

Pellis, S. and V. Pellis (2007), 'Rough and Tumble Play and the Development of the Social Brain', *Current Directions in Psychological Science* 16 (2): 95–8.

Pfaff, D. W. (2011), *Man & Woman: An Inside Story*, Oxford: Oxford University Press.

Picavet, C. and J. Reinders (2004), *Sexual Orientation and Young People*, Utrecht: The Netherlands: Colophon – Youth Incentives/Rutgers Nisso Groep.

Pinker, S. (2008), *Sexual Paradox*, New York: Scribner.

Poole, D. A. and M. A. Wolfe (2009), 'Child Development: Normative Sexual and Non-Sexual Behaviours that may be Confused with Symptoms of Sexual Abuse', in K. Kuehnle and M. Connell (eds), *The Evaluation of Child Sexual*

Abuse Allegations: A Comprehensive Guide to Assessment and Testimony, Hoboken, NJ: John Wiley & Sons Inc.

Preves, S. E. (2005), *Intersex and Identity – The Contested Self*, New Brunswick, NJ: Rutgers University Press.

Rampton, M. (2008), 'The Three Waves of Feminism', *Magazine of Pacific University* 14 (2). Available online: http://www.pacificu.edu/magazine_ archives/2008/fall/echoes/feminism.cfm (accessed 29 October 13).

Renold, E. (2005) *Girls, Boys and Junior Sexualities*, Oxon: RoutledgeFalmer.

Reynolds, M. A. and D. L. Herbenick (2003), 'Using Computer-Assisted Self-Interview (CASI) for Recall of Childhood', in J. Bancroft (ed.), *Sexual Development in Childhood*, Bloomington, IN: Indiana University Press.

Reynolds, M. A., D. L. Herbenick and J. Bancroft (2003), 'The Nature of Childhood Sexual Experiences', in J. Bancroft (ed.), *Sexual Development in Childhood*, Bloomington, IN: Indiana University Press.

Rich, P. (2012), 'Recognizing Healthy and Unhealthy Sexual Development in Children', in *WeldWaits*, online advice service, Weld County Government. Available online: http://www.weldwaits.com/assets/759dbb2b119Aa130B1A7. pdf (accessed 19 May 2015).

Rich-Harris, J. (1999), *The Nurture Assumption*, New York: Touchstone.

Riley, J. G. and R. B. Jones (2005), 'Investigating Gender Differences in Recess Play', *PlayRights* XXVI (1): 18–21.

Rind, B, P. Tromovitch and R. Bauserman (1998), 'A Meta-Analytic Examination of Assumed Properties of Child Sexual Abuse Using College Samples', *Psychological Bulletin* 124 (1): 22–53.

Rogers, C. and J. Sawyer (1998), 'Play in the Lives of Children, Washington, National Association for the Education of Young Children', in I. Cole-Hamilton, A. Harrop and C. Street, *The Value of Children's Play and Play Provision: A Systematic Review of the Literature*. London: New Policy Institute.

Rosenthal, R. (1963) 'On the Social Psychology of the Psychological Experiment: The Experimenter's Hypothesis as Unintended Determinant of Experimental Results', *American Scientist* 51 (2): 268–283: Sigma xi The Scientific Research Society. Available online: http://www.jstor.org/stable27838693 (accessed 30 December 2014).

Rubin, G. (1979), 'The Traffic in Women', *Toward an Anthropology of Women*, New York: Monthly Review Press.

Rush, E. and A. La Nauze, (2006), *Corporate Paedophilia – Sexualisation of Children in Australia*, Discussion paper No. 90, The Australia Institute.

Russell, W. (2005), *The Unnatural Art of Playwork*, Therapeutic Playwork Reader (2000–5), Ludemos Associates.

Rutter, M. (2006), 'Implications of Resilience Concepts for Scientific Understanding', *Annals of the New York Academy of Science* 1094: 1–12.

Sandfort, T. G. M. and J. Rademakers (2000), *Childhood Sexuality*, New York: Haworth Press.

Sax, L. (2005), *Why Gender Matters*: New York: Broadway Books.

Schuhrke (2000), 'Formation of Sexuality in Childhood', in *Marriage and Family Encyclopaedia*. Available online: http://family.jrank.org/pages/1537/Sexuality-in-Childhood-Formation-Sexuality-in-Childhood.html (accessed 13 May 2015).

Scott, S. L. (n.d.), 'What Makes Serial Killers Tick: Monsters or Victims'.
    Available online: http://kuijp.home.xs4all.nl/literature/WMSKT.pdf (accessed 4
    June 2015).
Servin, A., A. Nordsenstrum, A. Larsson and G. Bohlin (2003), 'Prenatal
    Androgens and Gender Typer Behaviour: A Study of Girls with Mild and
    Severe Forms of Congenital Adrenal Hyperplasia', *Developmental Psychology*
    39 (3): 440–50.
Seth, J. (2012), 'Playworkers as Epiguardians of the Genome?', in P. Else (ed.),
    Conference Report for Beauty of Play; Beauty Play, Essence, Sheffield: Ludemos.
Shibley-Hyde, J. (2005), 'The Gender Similarities Hypothesis',
    American Psychologist Vol. 60 Issue 6. Available online: http://www.
    areerpioneernetwork.org/wwwrook/user (accessed 9 April 2014).
Skelton, C. (2001), *Educating the Boys: Masculinities and Primary Education*,
    Maidenhead: Open University Press.
Smith, P. K. (2005), 'Play', in B. J. Ellis and D. F. Bjorklund (eds), *Origins of the
    Social Mind: Evolutionary Psychology and Child Development*, New York:
    Guilford Press.
Smith, P. K. (2010), *Children and Play*, Chichester: Wiley-Blackwell.
Spinka, M., R. Newberry and M. Bekoff (2001), 'Mammalian Play: Training for
    the Unexpected', *The Quarterly Review of Biology* 76 (2): 141–68.
Sutton, L., N. Smith, C. Dearden and S. Middleton (2007), *A Child's Eye View of
    Play*: Cambridge MA, Harvard University Press.
Sutton-Smith, B. (1997), *The Ambiguity of Play*, New Haven, CT: Harvard
    University Press.
Sutton-Smith, B. (2003), 'Play as a Parody of Emotional Vulnerability', in J. L.
    Roopnarine (ed.), *Play and Educational Theory and Practice, Play and Culture
    Studies*, 5. Westport, CT: Praeger.
Tannen, D. (1992), *You Just Don't Understand*, London, Virago Press.
Thomson, S. (2005), '"Territorialising" the Primary School Playground:
    Deconstructing the Geography of Playtime', *Children's Geographies* 3: 67–78.
Thorne, B. (1993/2009), *Gender Play – Girls and Boys in School*, Berkshire: Open
    University Press.
Thorne, B. and Z. Luria (1986), 'Sexuality and Gender in Children's Daily
    Worlds', *Social Problems* 33 (3): 176–90.
UNICEF (2010), *Working for an Equal Future – Policy on Gender Equality and
    the Empowerment of Girls and Women*, UNICEF.
United Nations (2013), *General Comment No. 17, The Right of the Child to Rest,
    Leisure, Play, Recreational Activities, Cultural Life and the Arts (Article 31)*,
    International Committee on the Rights of the Child. Available online: http://
    www.iccp-play.org/documents/news/UNGC17.pdf (accessed 9 April 2015).
Voon, V., T. B. Mole, P. Banca, L. Porter, L. Morris, et al. (2014), 'Neural
    Correlates of Sexual Cue Reactivity in Individuals with and without Compulsive
    Sexual Behaviours', *PLOS ONE*, 10.1371. Available online: http://journals.plos.
    org/plosone/article?id=10.1371/journal.pone.0102419 (accessed 3 June .2015).
Walkerdine (1989) 'The Regulation of Girls' in W. C. Harrison and J.
    Hood-Williams, *Beyond Sex and Gender*, London: Sage Publications Ltd.
Walkerdine (2004), 'Developmental Psychology and The Study of Childhood',
    in M. Kehilly, (ed.), *An Introduction to Childhood Studies*, Berkshire: Open
    University Press.

Waller, A, (2010), 'Revisiting Childhood Landscapes: Revenants of Druid's Grove and Narnia', *The Lion and the Unicorn* V34 (3), September: 303–19

Walliams, D. (2010), *The Boy in the Dress*, London: HarperCollins.

Whiting, B. and C. Edwards (1988), *Children of Different Worlds: The Formation of Social Behaviour*, Cambridge, MA: Harvard University Press.

Wingrave, Mary (2014), 'An Old Issue in a New Era: "Early Years Practitioners' Perceptions of Gender"', Doctoral thesis: University of Glasgow.

Wood, A. and Kilvington, J. (2011), 'Sex Differences, Sexuality and Gender Identity – What's Play Got To Do With It?', Paper for the International Play Association Conference: Cardiff, Wales.

Woolley, H. T. (1914), 'The Psychology of Sex', *Psychological Bulletin* 11: 353–79.

Yun, A., K. Bazar, A. Gerber, P. Lee and S. Daniel (2005), 'The Dynamic Range of Biological Functions and Variations of Many Environmental Cues may be Declining in the Modern Age: Implications for Diseases and Therapeutics', *Medical Hypotheses* 65: 173–8.

Zerzan, J. (n.d.), 'Patriarchy, Civilization and The Origins Of Gender', The Anarchist Library. Available online: http://theanarchistlibrary.org/library/john-zerzan-patriarchy-civilization-and-the-origins-of-gender (accessed 7 January 2014).

INDEX

CPSIA information can be obtained
at www.ICGtesting.com
Printed in the USA
LVOW10*2338150318

570084LV00007B/108/P